D0998556

LANDLORD AND PEASANT IN CHINA

A STUDY OF THE AGRARIAN CRISIS IN SOUTH CHINA

By

CHEN HAN-SENG

Member of Research Committee,
China Institute of Pacific Relations

With a Preface by
FREDERICK V. FIELD

Secretary, American Council, Institute of Pacific Relations

HYPERION PRESS, INC.
WESTPORT, CONNECTICUT

Library of Congress Cataloging in Publication Data

Ch'ên, Han-shêng, 1897–
    Landlord and peasant in China.

    Reprint of the 1936 ed. published by International
Publishers, New York.
    1. Land tenure—China. 2. Agriculture—Economic
aspects—China. 3. Farm tenancy—Economic aspects—
China. I. Title.
HD865.C5 1973   333.5'3'0951   73–866
ISBN 0-88355-062-8

Published in 1936 by International Publishers, New York

First Hyperion reprint edition 1973

Library of Congress Catalogue Number 73-866

ISBN 0-88355-062-8

Printed in the United States of America

PREFACE

IT IS AN unfortunate truism of our times that we do not act quickly upon the facts and information brought forward by social scientists. We have at hand far more knowledge than we make use of. Faced with acute social situations we are all too likely to succumb to wishful thinking, to fasten on those parts of the picture with which we are in sympathy to the exclusion of the other parts and of the whole, to keep our noses so close to the scene that we cannot view it in historical perspective. Perhaps large sections of society are frightened by what there is to be seen and in consequence consciously or unconsciously turn their eyes away to the dream world of an acquisitive society.

Perhaps nowhere is this more true than in the realm of international affairs. There the game of sophistry has been an easy one for commercial opportunists to play. For it is only recently—in this country a matter of less than two decades—that significant portions of the public have become aware of some of the factors involved, and even today the system of democratic government has not extended directly to foreign relations except through the Senatorial power of veto. And within this ill-lighted realm, China has remained more than usually obscure. Felt for emotionally at the level of sentiment, regarded reverently for the age of its civilization, considered a thing of mystery beyond practical Occidental understanding, sought after with lust by profit seekers, China is scarcely *understood* by Americans.

iii

This is not because the means for understanding it—at least in large part—are not at hand. It is because we have not made use of the knowledge and data at our disposal. It is because facts which speak for themselves are not heard. Dr. Chen Han-seng's study which follows is a case in point which I hope may prove the contrary. Here is a work of extraordinary importance and timeliness. It deals with the key to the socio-economic complex of China, the land problem; that is, the use to which the land is put, the ownership of it, tenancy, rent and other forms of taxation, and the effects of these phenomena on the people who live on the land. It deals with a question around which Chinese history—and indeed world history—is revolving. Dr. Chen presents facts which we accept as accurate either because of his own very high standing as a scholar or by comparison with other rural surveys which have been made in China. He draws certain inferences from these facts, some direct, some more remote. These inferences, being interpretations, cannot be verified with the same objectivity as can the facts on which they are based. But they can, nevertheless, be checked against the other things we know about China, about social and economic and political evolution, and about the forces and counter-forces which are involved in the Chinese equation. Dr. Chen's book, *if made use of,* will greatly advance our understanding of China and of the American relation to the Far Eastern situation.

Some of us will agree the whole way with Dr. Chen's interpretation and prognostication. Others of us will stop somewhere between the facts and what the author believes to be their ultimate meaning. What he has to say will not be easy for some to stomach, nonetheless it may be true. Conversely, others will be greatly pleased at the course of events he foresees, and to these I may suggest a particularly careful check on wishful thinking. But regardless of our presuppositions or inclinations, unless we can put this sort of study to social use, unless we can apply its conclusions, or else refute them in an equally scientific way, we are denying the whole intellectual basis of social action.

FREDERICK V. FIELD.

New York, May 30th, 1936.

CONTENTS

v

ACKNOWLEDGEMENTS

The author is indebted to the Sun Yat-sen Institute and to Lingnan University, Canton for financial aid—the first in connection with the field investigation for this study, and the other in connection with the publication of this record of the findings. He also desires to acknowledge with gratitude the editorial and other assistance rendered by Mr. Bruno Lasker and Mr. W. L. Holland of the international research staff of the Institute of Pacific Relations. The help of these institutions and individuals does not imply, however, that any of them assume responsibility for statements of fact or opinion contained in this report.

CHEN HAN-SENG.

INTRODUCTION

THIS study concerns itself with Kwangtung Province, not only because of the intrinsic local importance of agrarian distress in that region but because this region shows most clearly the effects of imperialist economic penetration on rural life and the growth of class antagonisms in China itself. The province has some thirty-two million of population, the density being about twice that of France. It is one of the richest provinces, with fruits of various kinds, sugar cane, camphor, rubber, and other tropical products in addition to the principal cereal cup-rice. Vegetation grows more luxuriantly here than in any other part of China; the land is so intensively cropped that, except on the upland areas, rice is harvested two or three times a year; here the mulberry leaves are gathered seven or eight times during the year. Kwangtung has one of the best highway systems in China. In less than a year, with the Hankow-Canton Railway completed, its trade area will extend—so far as physical equipment is concerned—not only to the Yangtze Valley but also to the Tibetan Plateau.

In spite of this comparative wealth for reasons which this study will attempt to clarify, labour power is being lost at an alarming rate. Labour in South China is sometime jokingly spoken of as the principal "export commodity", since the remittance of part of the wages of emigrant workers from abroad constitutes one of the main money incomes of this part of China. Back in the obscurity of more than a thousand years ago, Kwangtung was not only the first part of the country to carry on an overseas trade—first with the Arabs, then with the Portuguese, and finally with the British and other Western people—but millions of Kwangtung peasants have emigrated abroad. Most of the merchants, tin miners, and labourers on tobacco, sugar, and rubber plantations in British Malaya and Netherlands Indies, and most of the Chinese merchants, Chinese coolies, Chinese cooks, and Chinese laundry men in Australia and the Americas have come from this southernmost part of China. The rural situation here has been constantly compelling them to leave their homeland. But in recent times the discouragement of labour on the land of their fathers has become for these peasant people something more than an occasion for temporary labour overseas. It has taken on dimensions under which the land itself is in danger of losing its wealth-producing qualities, because its productivity can no longer be maintained. Not only will immigration restrictions, already severe in most of the countries to which Chinese have gone in the past, cut off what is left of this old safety valve for the constant population pressure of this region, but the pressure itself will increase as the ancient heritage, the land itself, deteriorates, and the privilege to cultivate it, to live with and on and from it, dwindles away. In the future, unless the agrarian problem is reasonably well solved, a new phase for both population movement and foreign trade must undoubtedly merge, with ominous consequences not only for China but also for the world at large.

Had there been an industrial development in China with its tempo and extent such as occurred in the United States of America before 1930, or such as was witnessed in the Soviet Union after that year, these rural proletariats and semi-proletariats in Kwangtung would not have gone to those distant European colonies to give up their bodies. The truth of the matter is that this artificial over-population has been inevitably created by a land monopoly without sufficient industrialization. In Kwangtung one-third of the peasant families possess less than five mow each, nearly half of the peasant families are entirely landless, and more than 60% of all the land cultivated is rented from landlords. The system of community land, especially the clan land in southernmost China, only aggravates the monopolistic situation. About 80% of the

Kwangtung peasants live together by their clans, because of their original tie to the clan land. Even today, of the total of 42,000,000 Mow of cultivated land in the province, 35% is the area of clan land and other kinds of public land. The annual rent of clan land in Kwangtung amounts to 126,000,000 Yuan; such a huge income from rent plus its annual interest, often doubles the combined income of both provincial and national revenues of Kwangtung. Such a powerful influence exerted by collective landlordism is not to be found in the history of landlordism in any European country.

Under such a monopolistic system of agricultural land, we must think of tax and rent as fundamentally of the same character; most of the taxes are being directly and indirectly extorted from the farm land and assessed according to its size. The land tax in Kwangtung has been greatly increased by two new policies. The first is the recent extensive building of public roads, with the pretext of improving rural communications but primarily for facilitating military movements. The second is the reorganization of village administration under the beautiful name of rural self-government; however, it is chiefly for furthering the purpose of taxation. Within the past five years the total tax burden has trebled, and this burden is being largely shifted upon the shoulders of peasants who have to pay rent. The rent, which is usually paid in grain, amounts to 50-57% of the entire harvest. No one can mistake this for a capitalistic rent. Such a high rent, together with all its consequent burdens, crushes the peasant and sends him to the usurer. In any one district of the province, 60-90% of all the peasant families are in debt. Many peasants have to seek a loan in grain; others have to pawn their clothes, furniture, and even hoes, rakes, harrows, ploughs, etc. The usual interest charged on a loan in grain is 30% for six months; the monthly interest of the pawn shop is 2 to 3%; sometimes as high as 6%. No one can think of such high rates of interest as being capitalistic, or possible in any capitalistic country. The bankrupted peasants rapidly give up their land through the process of mortgage; as landless peasants not taken in or "absorbed" by industry are ever on the increase, wages in general are falling down, and rents in all forms are rising. Thus, bankruptcy repeats itself and accelerates the process, till the speed of rural proletarization, or in China to be more exact, the speed of pauperization, far exceeds that of peasant exodus and possible industrialization. The present system of land monopoly in China can only bestow perpetual ownership to a selected few, and simultaneously force perpetual indebtedness upon an ever growing mass.

As it is clear, in this land monopoly it is rent and not capital that sways the entire economy. The non-capitalistic relations prevailing in China are further reflected and registered in the extreme smallness of the farm unit. This inadequate size of cultivation physically excludes the possibilities of rural credit and hinders the free play of capital itself. Of course the mere size of a farm cannot tell whether agriculture is capitalistic or pre-capitalistic. The criterion should rather be the content and condition of production, such as the nature of the crop, implements, fertilizers, intensity of labour power, etc. Thus in the United States the farm unit in the north is smaller than in the south, but capitalistic agriculture is certainly more developed in the north. Though since the Civil War the size of the farm in the south has been considerably reduced, southern agriculture has become more capitalistic. For here, after the reduction of the cultivated area, there comes a higher percentage of labour power in the total cost of production. But the situation in China is entirely different. Though the remnant of primitive commune farming is fast disappearing, though the patriarchal self-subsistence farming in many interior regions is also crumbling down, individual rural entrepreneurs pursuing a capitalistic farming are very rare; the dominating form of Chinese agriculture is still that of farming for simple commercial production. Owing to the exorbitant charge of rent, the poor and middle peasants cannot secure adequate land to employ all their available labour power, and to make full use of even their antiquated implements. In Kwangtung even the rich peasants cultivate only 25 Mow per family or less than 4 Mow per working person. The average cultivation per family among the middle peasants is 12 Mow, and among the poor peasants less than 6 Mow. Taking the peasantry as a whole, only 1% cultivates more than 50 Mow per family, 29% from 5 to 10 Mow, and no less than 43% cultivates not more than 5 Mow. A vast majority of the peasantry, all of the poor peasants and a good many of the middle peasants, are actually pining away on tiny plots of land.

On such ridiculously small farms, the producers can only curse the evils of commercial agriculture, but can never attain a real capitalistic development.

When we say that the Chinese agrarian economy is not yet capitalistic, we must not mistake it, however, as being still purely feudalistic. No one can deny the fact that for ages already the mode of classical feudalism in China has been distorted. As early as five centuries before the Christian era, extensive internal trade and various practices of usury fostered the growth of a new economic organism, a commercial agriculture, which witnessed the beginning of an interplay of forces: rent, tax, price and interest. The landlords who live on rent, the bureaucrats and militarists who live on taxes of the most diversified nature, the traders and compradores who live on the manipulation of prices, and the usurers who live on exorbitant interests, have become interlocking, even more so than the directors of modern monopolistic capital. But the money accumulated by these people, just like the money remitted home from the overseas Chinese, has been largely and preferably turned into land purchases. This process of land concentration can only perpetuate a pre-capitalistic system of agrarian economy.

Modern international trade had been carried on in Kwangtung for nearly one hundred years before the Yangtze ports were set up to trade with western capitalistic nations. From the middle of the 18th Century to the middle of the 19th, Canton was practically the only place in China open for foreign commerce; all the imports of opium and cloth and all the exports of tea and silk went through the hands of Hong Merchants. These Hong people in Canton, the forerunners of a like type, the present-day compradores, flourishing in Amoy and Ningpo, in Shanghai and Hankow, and in Tientsin, feverishly piled up their wealth through commissions and squeeze. Perhaps the most illustrious Hong man was Howqua, whose full name was Wo E-woo (1769-1843); in his honour the British firm of Jardine, Matheson and Company has taken its Chinese name E-woo. According to the *Indian Mail* (London, Jan. 6, 1844, p. 264), "he has left about 26,000,000 dollars, the fruit of his own industry, to his two sons, the eldest only sixteen". But this enormous accumulation has dwindled away; much of it has been used for land purchases and for rent collection.

Foreign commerce has undoubtedly accelerated the accumulation
of wealth, which under Chinese conditions, only aggravates land
concentration. Of all Chinese provinces Kwangtung has been
subjected to the influence of international trade the longest time;
it is no wonder that of all the fertile regions of the country,
Kwangtung has gone the greatest distance in class differentiation.

It is well known to all students of modern Chinese history that
foreign commerce has brought in its train far-reaching influences
of the industrial capital. The increasing imports of factory
manufactured articles has wrought the decline of handicraft industries all over China. The metal worker, whether iron, copper,
tin or silver, the potter and tile-maker, the painter and furniture-
maker, the tailor and tanner, the rope-maker and wood-carver,
and especially the silk-reeler and cotton-weaver, all have had their
future narrowed and eclipsed by the onslaught of modern industrial goods, most of them being foreign. This means an ever
decreasing income from household production, or from the auxiliary
work of the peasantry. During the World War, hand-weaving
witnessed a sudden revival, because the prices of imported textiles
had been advanced by war conditions. At that time, there were,
for instance, nearly ten thousand peasant women at the hand looms
in one single town of Fatshan, in the district of Nan-hai. But
now China is receiving all the effects of dumping from capitalistic
nations in the midst of their own economic crisis. The prices of
imported textiles in Kwangtung have dropped in the last few
years by more than half; handweaving therefore can no longer
maintain itself. In addition to a drastic wage cut of the Fatshan
weavers, about eight thousand women have been thrown out
of work. The unemployed in the towns are now being driven
back again towards the countryside, from where they have originally come. Certainly, under the present circumstances, modern
trade is intensifying the process of rural pauperization on a gigantic
scale hitherto unheard of.

Back in the Seventies of the last century, after several Yangtze
ports had been opened to foreign commerce, Chinese trade and
usury capital no longer limited its sphere of operation to internal
markets but began to link itself with foreign commerce and industrial activities. Hence several powerful compradore organizations, such as the China Merchants Steamship Navigation

Company, have come into existence. In fact about this time, with the advance of foreign influences, a new type of bureaucrat, the compradore type, has sprung up. The first and most famous representative of this type was Li Hung-chang. Unlike his teacher and superior officer, Tseng Kuo-fang, who was still of the old and feudal type, he built up his ascendency in political and financial matters through the help of compradores and the assistance of foreigners; on more than one occasion he even acted as a compradore himself. He must be accredited also as the first bureaucrat who introduced modern military weapons in suppressing the successive peasant revolts. In this import of foreign arms and ammunitions we may trace perhaps the most dreadful effect brought by industrial capital upon the Chinese rural life. The expeditions which have quelled the Taipings in the Yangtze provinces, the Mohammedans in the upper Yellow River valley, the Boxers in Hopei, Shantung and Honan, and other minor disturbances, testify that the secret of success lies in the ability and opportunity of utilizing destructive instruments furnished by the Western arsenals. When Li Hung-chang was viceroy in Kwangtung, at the time of the Boxers, the Canton government was Hongkong's as well as Macao's best customer for munitions; but he urgently requested the British and Portuguese authorities to refrain from selling the same to "the potential wrong-doers".

On the basis of imported military weapons, a modern army has been gradually built up in China. But due to the remnants of feudalistic relationship, the commanders of new troops simply constitute themselves as a group of militarists who are often simultaneously landlords and compradores. Yuan Shi-kai was the first and most famous representative of the Chinese militarists. After him a host of big and little warlords, countless as the stars, have spread throughout the provinces. A new type of landlord is rising from among these militarists, fattened as they are from tax incomes, loan commissions, and squeezes from soldiers' payments. These new landlords are far more powerful than the landlords who belong to the old gentry, because they can now collect their rents more effectively by direct force. It is said that in Kwangtung, every division general, nearly every brigade general, and even most of the regimental lieutenants, possess large tracts of land in their home or neighboring districts. Whenever and wherever such land purchases are being made, and these are always extraordinary large transactions, the land price and consequently also the rent tend to rise generally. Thus a new wave of land concentration is going on. In Meu-ming, for instance, one division general who is still serving in the Kwangtung provincial army, receives from his land possession a total amount of rent every year something like 1,800 piculs of unhusked rice; the entire rent yielded by all the private land of this district aggregates not more than 682,000 piculs. Many people know that a military chief in Kwangtung owns real estate property in Hongkong to the value of 20,000,000 Yuan; but few have learned the fact that this same son of Mars also enjoys an immense domain of agricultural land in his home district. This district happens to border French Indo-China, and since his land extends over the national boundary, he is paying land tax to the colonial government of France.

The militarists with their subordinate bureaucrats are constantly demanding more and more taxes and loans, in order to make new purchases of arms and ammunitions, which are absolutely necessary to them for suppressing the peasant revolts and for maintaining themselves in power. As the tax burden and consequently the rent becomes more and more oppressive, as the financial and political measures taken by the militarists and bureaucrats assumes more and devastating proportions, the magnitude of peasant bankruptcy is enlarging constantly. Before the wide-spreading revolts of the bankrupted peasants as well as the middle peasants who do not have enough land to work upon, the ruling class, with whom all those who wish to maintain the *status quo* are in sympathy, can find its last defensive means only in the superior military weapons imported from capitalistic nations. Thus since the middle of last century, revolts—munitions—taxes, or, taxes—munitions—revolts have whirled themselves into a vicious circle. Of course, China is not the only country where life consists of vicious circles and the progress of breaking them. But under the present conditions, China as a whole is not making any progress in this respect. This may be illustrated by the most recent case of Kiangsi, a province immediately north of Kwangtung. Professor C. Dragoni of Rome, accredited on a mission to the Nanking government on the recommendation of the League of Nations in 1933, has made the following observations. In the regions of Kiangsi recovered from the Communists, the present authorities "try to re-establish the former owners in possession in every case where it is possible to do so. For this purpose, they admit that ownership can be proved not only in the normal way, *e.g.* by deeds and documents, but also in much more simple and informal ways. This happens not only when boundary lines are preserved, but also when they have been completely destroyed". "What renders matters worse is that the Committees (of Rural Reconstruction) are recruited from the gentry, who naturally will be disposed to act in the interests of their class and not in the interests of the smaller people. The latter will certainly be in a worse plight than they were before the Communist occupation. On the whole, not only will the old system come back, with all its defects, but a worse system will take its place". (Annexes to Report of League's Technical Delegate on his Mission in China, Nanking, April, 1939, p. 220-221).

Chinese militarists and bureaucrats, a great majority being themselves landlords and compradores, can never and will never help to liberate the peasants from their bondage. They only desire to keep up, as far as they possibly can, a status of land monopoly, which is the basis of their exploitation. In the eyes of foreign capitalists, however, they are almost indispensable as they are instrumental in "maintaining peace and order" and in making China "safe for trade". It is plain and inevitable that the imperialists, who urgently seek a profit as immediate as it can be, would not side with the revolting peasants, but would rather render a ready hand to assist the war-lords who are also landlords. Furthermore, since the general crisis of the capitalistic world has revealed its hideous face in China, the process of foreign military and financial invasion is being doubly quickened. Hence Chinese industrial capital is doomed to recede and decline; Chinese agriculture cannot expect a better fate. Even the rich peasants in China who, under American conditions such as found in the era of "Westward Movement", might be expected to develop a sort of capitalistic farming, are now diminishing their area of cultivation as well as their labour power. They cannot afford to run the risks which are almost sure to come from economic and political uncertainties. Also they cannot stand the onslaught of the ever increasing imports of agricultural products. In 1933 China had to receive food from abroad amounting to no less than a quarter of her total imports, not counting the huge quantities of smuggled sugar. Many of the Chinese rich peasants rather lease out a part of their land, to insure an easier and safer income from rent. Thus, an atavistic feature has to be reckoned with in the present Chinese agrarian economy. Those who started a few decades or even a few years ago as rural entrepreneurs, have now involuntarily surrendered themselves to a system of feudalistic exploitation.

Almost every one of these economists and historians who have studied the Chinese situation, has discerned therein an abundance of feudalistic remnants; but only a few scholars have not neglected the multiple colonial character in Chinese political economy, which is in fact contributing more than any other factor towards the tenacity, and even intensity, of the existing feudalistic relationship. The problems of China and India to-day are not as analogous to those of England and France before industrialization, as Professor R. H. Tawney has suggested in his *Land and Labour in China,* (London, 1932, pp. 78-79). The Chinese peasants are suffering from feudalism as well as from capitalism, from a crisis of underproduction in China and also from a crisis of overproduction abroad, and moreover, they are suffering as a colonial people under foreign domination. Even though we should take Prof. Tawney's view that the disorders of Chinese agriculture are acute in degree but not unique in kind, *e.g.* the disintegration of Chinese agrarian economy characteristically resembles the *ancien régime*, let us not forget the history of that great French Revolution which set free the French peasants from their feudalistic bondage. Undoubtedly, those who understand that which Professor Dragoni has correctly observed in the almost up-to-date case of Kiangsi, can no longer entertain any reformist moonshine for China.

In his report, *China and the Depression* (published as a Supplement to *The Economist*, London, May 19, 1934), Sir Arthur Salter, recently economic adviser to the Nanking government, sees China as a country in which the process of being "de-capitalized" is going on most rapidly; he sees China as a colony with an economic status much lower than India. His "modest ambition" is that "peace and order and wise direction" should help China soon to attain an Indian standard. On one hand, he realizes, "the foundation of China's economic life is, and must remain, her agricultural production. Her fundamental problem is to increase the farmers' production, whether by improving the conditions under which they produce food or by supplementary handicraft-work. Real industrial development must be based principally upon the farmers' purchasing power". On the other hand, he also recognizes "the very small margin of production over consumption", which at present is swiftly diminishing because of famine, war and taxation. The truth is that there is hardly any prospect for a land reform; and as we know, the future of Chinese handicraft industries is anything but bright. But Sir Arthur instinctively fears any sort of revolution, especially when it takes place in a colonial country. So, he is quite emphatic in his advice; he asserts that "China should proceed by stages—and not jump her stages". Will the Chinese peasants follow his advice and submit themselves further, or will they fight for their own interests, which after all are the interests of the nation and indeed of the world? The essence of the agrarian problem and of the agrarian crisis in China, is how a national liberation movement can be successfully conducted to abolish the basis of all colonial and feudalistic exploitations. For these exploitations prove to be the fundamental obstacle in developing agriculture in China to a higher level, and to raising the living of 400 million people to a higher standard. It is absolutely necessary to remove this obstacle, thereby liberating the productive forces of the country, and putting an end to the evils of "cheap Oriental labour"—necessary not only in the subjective sense of the word, but also in the objective sense, for the removal is inevitable, and no power on earth can prevent it.

CHEN HAN-SENG.

AGRARIAN PROBLEMS IN SOUTHERNMOST CHINA

CHAPTER I

DISTRIBUTION OF LAND OWNERSHIP AND USE

WITH an area five-sixths that of Great Britain, or almost half as large as that of France, Kwangtung has probably less than a third of its land area cultivable—according to the Liankwang Geological Survey, which also states that at present less than one-sixth of that land area is under cultivation. Most of the plateau regions and low but not steep hills have never been cultivated; even hilly places where terrace farming might be introduced are left barren. Such is the agricultural condition in Kwangtung. Yet, the industrial development of the province is far behind that of Kiangsu and Chekiang; the economy has to rely almost entirely upon agriculture as the source of revenue.

There are three principal reasons for this lack of industrialization in a region which, almost more than any other in China, has been exposed to contact with the outside world. First, enclosed by a ring of mountains, which cut it off from neighbouring provinces and, especially, from the large hinterland to the west, the market area available for any potential industry is too limited to invite large-scale investment, compared with the much greater market potentially available for an enterprising industrialist in the Yangtse Valley to the north. Second, the region is too near Hong Kong to compete with that colony which, in addition to the advantage of free trade, has as inexpensive an access to practically all parts of

Kwangtung, through water transportation, as has any Kwangtung city; and in addition, Hong Kong has, of course, the advantages of superior protection and a more stable currency. Third, and somewhat connected with the foregoing, is the handicap imposed upon industrial developments by war and political disturbance until about three years ago. While Chinese small-scale enterprise has to a remarkable degree overcome these and other handicaps, they are too serious to warrant any large investment in industrial ventures with slow returns.

The result of a survey covering 152 villages in 38 districts or *hsien*, shows that peasant families (including agricultural labourers) made up 85 per cent of the total population. (See table 1). The remaining 15 per cent of the population is composed, in the main, of merchants and officials, both active and retired, only to a small extent of artisans and others types of workers. The merchants and retired officials also are, for the most part, the landlords and the money-lenders of the community; in fact, their income from rent and interest on loans often greatly exceeds that from business profits or from returns on other forms of investment.

Even in the District of P'an-yu, nearest to the city of Canton, a district one would expect to be much more advanced in trade and manufacture, the agricultural population is still predominating. According to statistics obtained in 69 villages in this district, more than three-fourths of the population are peasant families. (See table 2a). In the District of Hwa-hsien, about thirty miles north of Canton, the proportion of agriculturists is almost the same as in the district of P'an-yu. Of the 10,321 families in 22 villages investigated, pure peasant families constitute more than three-fourths. Besides these, there are 600 families engaging in retail trade and agriculture simultaneously. (See table 2b). A large majority of the population have, therefore, to be supported by agricultural land, and yet vast tracts of cultivable land are not fully utilized. Much of this idle land has at one time been under cultivation; but today it is not even used for rough pasture or for forestry and if it is not eroded—as much of it is—produces only a coarse grass which constitutes the villagers' chief supply of fuel. Just what are the conditions that make for the decline of agricultural production or prevent its development, constitutes the main theme of our present study.

The fundamental causes of this situation can be explained only by examining the social relations in agricultural production. These relations, growing out of the natural conditions, determine not only the economic, social, and political setting but also the specific character and development of agricultural production. They include the relations between the producer, on the one hand, and, on the other, those who control the land, credit, material supplies—such as seed and fertilizer—the price of labour, the markets, and the policies of provincial and local government—the national government having very little direct influence on the every-day concerns of the people in a distant province.

Just as in the relations which govern industrial production the ownership and use of machines occupy the first and foremost place, so the ownership and use of land claim the most important position in those which govern agricultural production. It is of great significance, therefore, that the percentage of agricultural tenants in Kwangtung is one of the highest of all provinces in China. While no statistical survey of the entire province has yet been made, our data for many districts indicate the proportion of tenant families to the whole peasantry. For example, of the nine subdistricts of Chung-shan, four have from 70 to 90 per cent tenant families; again, of the nine subdistricts of the District of Hoh-pu, three have more than 90 per cent of tenants among their peasant families. In other districts investigated, the smallest proportion of tenants found among the peasant families was 70 per cent and the highest 90 per cent. In the 69 villages of Pan-yu investigated, 77 per cent of the peasantry are tenant families. (See table 2a). In the 22 villages of Hwa-hsien investigated, 73 per cent of the peasantry are tenant families. (See table 2b). According to information received through correspondence from 152 villages in 38 districts, tenant families make up 57 per cent of the total agricultural population (see table 1); apparently, the spread of ownership among the land users in these villages is comparatively large. There are, however, many other villages in Kwangtung with much higher percentages of tenancy. The home village of one of our investigators may be cited as an example. He comes from New-wan-hsiang, located in the sixth sub-district of Sin-hwei; of more than 3,500 peasant families in that village four-fifths are tenants.

3

The figures quoted so far do not show how many families possess no land. In addition to a majority of the tenant farmers, there are many hired agricultural labourers who do not own any land. In the ten villages investigated as representative of the District of Pan-yu, no less than 52 per cent of all the peasant families are either those of hired agricultural labourers or those of peasants absolutely landless. (See table 3). Five years before, this percentage was only 50; during this short period, the number of landless families in the peasantry of Pan-yu has increased by 3.5 per cent. Between 1928 and 1933, the peasant families in the ten representative villages of this district which have been investigated have increased in number from 50.3 per cent of the total number to 52.0 per cent.

While theoretically the ownership or part-ownership of land may be no indication of the relative well-being of the peasant and labouring classes, actually—as will be seen below where the production relations which prevail in this region are further analysed—under the present distribution of economic and political power in China, the landless peasant is little better off than a serf. The Chinese peasant is comparable, not with the *Bauer* of modern Europe or the "farmer" of English-speaking countries; but he resembles in status the peasant of other pre-capitalistic countries. He is farming for subsistence and not for profit. He thinks of himself not as of a man engaged in a business, but as closely related to the soil; and, since mobility in China has a very short range, this usually means the soil of his fathers. To lose his hold upon even a small portion of the common heritage of all, the land, is for the Chinese peasant the greatest calamity.

In our observation of the way in which the ownership of land is distributed, we should not, however, take the peasantry as a whole; we should, rather, endeavour to analyse it in its incidence as regards different classes of peasants. But how are we going to classify the peasant families? If we classify them according to the size of their land property, then we shall miss other important aspects of the social and economic relations, that affect production and consequently shall not be able to show the real economic status of the different types of family. If we classify them according to the relation of ownership and differentiate them as owners, part-tenants, and tenants, then we are again limited to a formal distinc-

4

tion which, from the point of view of welfare, may not be the only important one. In reality a family here classified as owners, if it has very little land of its own, will be obliged to send out its members to be hired labourers. To think of such a family primarily as a land-owning one would give a wrong slant on its status. Such a family may be poorer than a tenant family which cultivates much land, though owning very little or none of it, and hires a number of labourers. Even if we classify the peasant families according to the area of the land they cultivate, trying to determine the economic position by the size of the holding, such a classification would not be reliable as an indication of their economic status. The size of the holding shows only the area of cultivation, and may not show the magnitude of the farm business. For example, it makes a great deal of difference whether a holding of, say, five mow is devoted to taro or to rice; the money income from the one crop would be only a fraction of what the other brings in. On the other hand, the magnitude of the farm business by itself cannot either furnish a reliable basis for a really revealing classification. There are some big landlord families managing small orchards, vegetable lots, or a few mow of mulberries. Judging from the size of the holding they cultivate, we should most likely mistake them for poor peasant families; but nothing would be further from the truth, because most of their income comes from that part of their land which they lease out. Again, to compare a family which cultivates all of its own land with that of a tenant, both cultivating the same number of mow, the size of their holdings may be exactly the same, but obviously because one has to pay rent and the other has not, they are in a very different economic position.

In short, looking upon the economic status of these families only in relation to tenancy will not help us to establish meaningful categories in which to classify the different economic types of peasant families. This proves to be more evident in the agrarian economy of Kwangtung than in that of the provinces of the Yellow River Basin. An analysis of 923 peasant families in our ten representative villages of Pan-yu shows that as many as one in every six of the "rich peasants" (as defined in table 4 and more fully below, pp. 7) possess no land at all. These men can hardly be called "landless" agricultural labourers just because they own no land.

They are not employed for wages; on the contrary, they themselves hire agricultural labourers. There are other rich peasants who, though they own some land, own too little to suffice their farming business. We find, therefore, that almost one-half of the rich peasants in Pan-yu have to lease some land. Among the "middle" peasants whose income from agricultural sources, under our definition of the class, (table 4 and below, page 7) barely meets their ordinary expenditure, as many as three out of every five have to be tenants. Needless to say, an even greater majority among the "poor" peasants have to lease all the land they use: more than three-fourths of them are tenant families. (See table 5. For definition of class see table 4 and below, page 7).

The proportion of leased land to the total land area cultivated by the different classes in Pan-yu is over one-half for the rich peasants, seven-tenths for the middle peasants, and four-fifths for the poor peasants (table 6). If we exclude the vegetable gardens, where cultivation is comparatively intensive and the holdings are consequently smaller, and also the scattered orchard, where the land is comparatively hilly and where, because of the nature of the crop, the basis of profit is less secure—that is, if we only count the land generally under rice cultivation, the major crop for the whole area here under survey—then the proportion of land under tenancy would be even higher. Of the total area cultivated by the rich, the middle and the poor peasants, almost three-fourths is being rented (table 7). Even the rich peasants have to pay rent on more than three-fifths of the land they cultivate, since less than two-fifths belong to them.

There are 5,742 mow under tenancy in the ten representative villages of Pan-yu. A comparison between the percentages of families in the three classes of peasants and the percentages of leased land demonstrates very clearly not only the superior ability but also the actual practice of the rich peasants to lease land. The rich peasants, constituting 13 per cent of all the peasant families, lease 28 per cent of all the land under tenancy, while the poor peasants who make up more than 64 per cent of the peasant population lease only 44 per cent of that land.

The average area of rented land per family also differs for these three classes: it is only 4.7 mow for poor peasants, not more than 8.3 mow for middle peasants, but 15.1 mow for rich peasants. It

PERCENTAGE OF FAMILIES AND OF LEASED LAND AMONG
PEASANT CLASSES
(Ten Representative Villages in Pan-yu District, 1933)

Peasant Class	Families in Class	Leased Land
	Per Cent	Per Cent
Rich	12.7	28.2
Middle	23.0	27.7
Poor	64.3	44.1
Total	100.0	100.0

is to be noted, further, that the poor peasants lease less dry land which is cheaper in price but more difficult to manage; they lease more irrigated land which is dearer in price and higher in productivity. With the rich peasants, it is the other way around. (See table 8).

What does this mean? The poor peasants, pressed by their difficult livelihood, have to rent fertile land, as far as possible, in the hope for a relatively large income from each land unit; the rich peasants, on the other hand, often utilize their surplus capital to lease such dry lands which the poor peasants cannot use. Only the rich peasants can afford to undertake a form of production which involves a relatively large cost for land improvement. It is clear that what at first glance may appear as a similar transaction, namely the leasing of, say, five mow of land, may actually mean two very different things in two cases: in the one case the tenant goes to work on his land straight away and, with a minimum of expenditure, manages to get within a few months a crop of beans or rice which he can sell and apply toward his rent, with something left over to feed his family. The other faces a barren holding; before he can get any return, he has to fertilize; and this costs money and labour. The poor man cannot afford to lease such land as this; he has not the necessary means to invest and wait. The rich peasant, on the other hand, sees a special opportunity in leasing land of this sort on which he can use some of his surplus capital with the prospect of a fair return at a comparatively moderate rental. Surely, therefore, we cannot look upon the

7

tenancy relation alone as an adequate basis for classifying peasant families.

A more promising way to classify them is to regard livelihood as the basis. Livelihood here means land and labour, and this in quite specific aspects: the land is that which the family uses, and our concern is with the amount of that land and the conditions under which the family may use it; the labour is that which the family puts into the land or hires to use on the land. Taking that land and that labour as the two main points of reference for our classification, we have to find out, first, the average number of persons per family in the village and, second, the number of mow owned or rented which is necessary for its support. Since the rent is usually one-half of the produce, the size of the rented area may be counted as one-half that of the owned. When a peasant family is barely capable of self-support from the land, and in its agricultural labour not directly exploited by, nor exploiting, others, we may say that such a family belongs to the class of "middle peasants." The status of the middle peasants helps us to determine that of the other two classes of peasantry. When a peasant family hires one or more agricultural labourers by the year, or hires a number of labourers by the day or by the season during busy times, to an extent exceeding in its total consumption of labour power that required by the average middle-peasant family for self-support, or when the land which it cultivates surpasses in area the average of the land used by the middle peasant, we shall then classify this family as that of a "rich peasant." Where we see families cultivating twice as much land as the middle peasants in their village, we may safely classify such families also as those of rich peasants, without further considering the labour relations. The "poor peasants" are comparatively easy to recognize. All peasant families whose number of cultivated mow falls below that of the middle peasants, and whose members, besides living on the fruits of their own cultivation, have to rely upon a wage income or some income of an auxiliary nature, belong to the poor peasants in general. Those poor peasants who do not cultivate any land, either their own or leased, but hire themselves out, or who cultivate a mere patch of land but have to support themselves chiefly by selling their labour power in agriculture are called hired agricultural labourers, but still belong to the peasantry.

The status of the middle peasants in some of the villages of Pan-yu District may be illustrated by the following statistical facts:

COMPARATIVE STATUS OF MIDDLE PEASANTS
(Twelve Villages of Pan-yu District, 1932-33)

Village	Average Number of Persons Per Family (a)	Average Number of Mow Necessary for Living (b)	Number of Hired Labour Units Required for Harvest Season (c)
Mei-tien	4	6 (rice)	12
Lung-tien	4	6 (rice)	12
Pei-shan	5	6 (rice)	30
Sha-dien-kang	5	8 (rice)	30
Nan-pu	5	10 (rice)	20
Kiu-tseng	5	10 (rice)	20
Tang-yai	5	10 (rice)	10
Pei-tseng	5	3 (rice)	None hired if there are 2 full-time labourers at home.
Kang-sin	5	10 (rice)	20
Kwei-tien	.5	6 (rice) or 3 (vegetables)	20 (rice) or 75 (vegetables)
Ting-lung-fong	6	7 (rice)	5
Huang-pien	6	7 (rice) or 3 (vegetables) or 6 (fruit)	14 (rice) or 80 (vegetables) or 64 (fruit)

(a) A further refinement of this column, to state the size of the family in terms of male units, has not been found practicable and is unnecessary because practically all the members of these families take part, more or less, in the agricultural work.

(b) If the land is leased, and not owned, the areas here given have to be doubled, to allow for rent. The average area of land required which is given in this column depends for each village on the quality of the soil and on the nature of the predominant principal crop. In the absence of technical studies to establish such a standard, the estimates here given are based on the judgment of the most competent informants who could be found in each of the villages named.

(c) The average number of hired labour units, in terms of persons per day, required by a family of average size (as given in first column) to harvest each crop—there may be several crops a year—on a holding of average size (as given in the second column).

A comparison between the percentage of families in the different classes and that of their land possessions in the total cultivated area demonstrates the disparity of land distribution (see table 9): in the district of Pan-yu, rich peasants, constituting almost one-ninth of the peasant families, possess one-half of the land owned by the peasants. On the other hand, the poor peasants whose families number nearly three-fifths of the total, possess little more than one-fifth of the land. More than one-half of all the peasant families in this same district, as we have already seen (table 3), are entirely landless. Less than one-tenth of the peasant families possess more than 30 mow each; one-third of them possess less than 5 mow each. Of the rich peasant families, one-sixth have more than 20 mow each, but of the middle and the poor peasants not a single family possesses more than 20 mow. One half of all the middle peasant families possess less than 5 mow each; and fully three-fifths of the poor peasant families possess no land at all. (See table 10). Again, if we wish to know the average number of mow owned per family, the statistics from Pan-yu shows us: it is less than 1 mow among the poor peasants and the agricultural labourers; less than 4 mow even among the middle peasants; and it is only among the rich peasants that it reaches 11 mow. (See table 11).

This concentration of land ownership is of no obvious theoretical significance in itself for the relative prosperity of the different peasant classes. That significance arises from the special conditions of land holding in China in relation to the exercise of economic and political power. As we shall further see below, the landless peasant and the peasant who has to lease a large part of his holding are exposed to exploitation of various kinds much more than is the owner. On the other hand, the owner, by having control of an essential means of livelihood, has in this densely populated region a power which he would not possess under other circumstances. A growing concentration of land ownership in China always has been a symptom of growing distress. At present, and in the region under survey, it is intensified by political insecurity and economic depression. Excessive taxation, scarcity of credit, loss of markets, and, to a lesser extent, the closing of labour opportunities but recently open overseas, all contribute to a growth of the disparity between need for land and land ownership here noted.

Only five years before, the average number of mow possessed by each peasant family was higher. During this short period it has been reduced among all classes of peasants. (See table 12). With the rich peasants the decrease of land possession has been 4.2 per cent; with the poor and the hired peasants it has been 4.4 per cent; and with the middle peasants it has been as much as 5.8 per cent. The comparative degree of decrease is not without significance. That the middle peasants lose their land faster than the other classes simply reflects the accelerating process of inequality itself. The poor peasant who still owns a little land hangs on to it with desperation.

Disparity is not confined to the distribution of land possession but is to be found also in the proportion of total area of land cultivated by the different classes. These proportions are certainly incongruous with the number of the cultivators in each class and reflect, not the need for land, but the respective ability to command means of production. The more affluent peasants not only can afford to lease more land; they also can pay more wages—to say nothing of purchases of fertilizer and their ability to finance improvements, such as drainage, which do not yield immediate returns. Furthermore, only the rich peasants can take extra land for such commercial crops as fruit which require much investment and a longer period before there is any return on the capital. The rich peasants, constituting less than one-eighth of the families, have the use of one-third of the cultivated land. At the other extreme, little more than another third is all the land which the poor peasants have at their disposal, although they and their families make up two-thirds of the peasant population. (See table 13). Even among the rich peasants themselves, not even one out of every ten families cultivates more than 50 mow; and such a family is not to be found among the middle and the poor peasants. Among the middle peasants, nine-tenths of the families cultivate less than 20 mow each; and among the poor peasants, about an equal proportion of the families cultivate less than 10 mow each. (See table 14). Not counting the hired agricultural labourers, nearly three-fourths of the entire peasantry in Pan-yu cultivate on the average less than 10 mow per family. The average cultivated area per family is 25.5 mow for the rich peasants, 11.7 mow for the middle peasants, and 5.7 mow for the poor peasants. (See table 15).

By referring back to the estimates of land required for the sustenance of life, given on page 9, it will be found that the average cultivated holding of 5.7 mow for poor peasants is far below the average requirement, especially if we take into account the fact that this holding is almost all leased, so that, according to our estimate, the required minimum of cultivated area per family should be doubled to allow for the rent that must be paid. Even the average cultivated holding of 11.7 mow for middle peasants apparently barely meets the minimum requirement of subsistence in most villages, since many of the peasants of this class also have to lease some or all of their land; and in a few villages this average of 11.7 mow evidently falls below the minimum requirement. If we were to take into account the hired agricultural labourers with their families—who, after all, must also be sustained from the total cultivated area—the average holding of 9.6 mow per family would be correspondingly reduced by approximately 9 per cent, which is the proportion of the labourers' families in the total peasant population. The tiny patches which these agricultural laborers lease and cultivate are of negligible proportion in the total cultivated area.

According to the statistics of the ten representative villages of Pan-yu, 68 per cent of the cultivated land is under rice; 17 per cent under rotating crops of wheat, cotton, taro, and peanuts; 13 per cent under fruits; and 2 per cent under commercial vegetable crops. (See table 16). Rice occupies 68.4 per cent of all the land cultivated by the rich peasants; 70.6 per cent of that cultivated by the middle peasants; and 65.4 per cent of that cultivated by the poor peasants. (See table 17). The explanation of this difference is that the rich peasants are in a better position to raise more valuable commercial crops, while the poor peasants have more land of a poor grade on which other food crops, such as taro, yield a more reliable subsistence. The middle peasant, however, relies upon his rice crop above all, both for the feeding of his family and for cash. Undoubtedly, rice is the chief agricultural product of Pan-yu, as well as of the entire province of Kwangtung. A wrong notion has been entertained by not a few people, that since rice needs more intensive cultivation than wheat, it is only rational to maintain the rice cultivation on a smaller scale. An economy of small holdings is ideal for that crop, they hold. It is true, of course, in certain particular regions that the net income per land unit of intensive agriculture is greater than that of extensive agriculture; but if the necessary production costs and the necessary labour power per land unit are taken into account, it can readily be proved that a larger-scale agriculture is superior to a smaller. There is scientific evidence to this effect from a number of sources. In California where, of course, the cost of labour is an even more serious factor than it is in the Far East, the sowing of rice is done by airplane over large acreages, and with production on a scale which no one would attempt in the Far East the price has been kept down to a level at which the local crop not only competes successfully with rice imports but could until recently, when an import embargo was imposed in Japan, be in large part exported to that country and sold in its markets.

As there is not yet available a true budgetary study of land holdings of different sizes in Kwangtung, we may in this connection refer to the result of an investigation among the rice peasants in Japan. A preliminary report by the farm management section of the Japanese Imperial Agricultural Association has been published in the *Tokyo Asahi Shimbun* (page 4, morning issue, June 28 1934). This report resulted from an investigation of 900 rice peasant families who own the land they cultivate. Among these families the average cost of rice production per tan per family is as follows:—

Area of Cultivation	Direct Cost of Production	Indirect Cost of Production	Total Cost of Production
Below 5 tan	¥37.00	¥32.00	¥69.00
5 tan to 1 cho*	34.00	33.00	67.00
2½ to 3 cho	33.00	27.00	60.00
Above 5 cho	29.00	19.00	48.00

* 10 tans or about 16 mow.

Thus, according to the cost of production per land unit, the larger the area of cultivation, the less expensive is the means of producing. Seeds, fertilizers, labour animals, and agricultural wages constitute the direct costs of production. Tax, interest, house, implements, and fees for land improvement are considered indirect costs of production. There are two reasons why some of these costs are lower per unit for the larger holding: some costs— that of tools, for example, of sheds, threshing floor, and the like— are simply spread over more units of cultivated area; others are diminished by substitution, such as that of animal for human labour power. In case the area of cultivation is larger, then the number of labour animals per unit is greater, and hence the quantity of home-made fertilizers available is also proportionately

13

greater. The Japanese association states that among families each cultivating less than 5 tan, only 48 per cent use home-made fertilizers; but among families each cultivating more than 5 cho (50 tan) as many as 56 per cent make their own fertilizers.

It may be objected that rice cultivation in Japan differs too much from that in Kwangtung to permit of a revealing comparison. The writer has been assured, however, that, so far as this sample study is concerned, the conditions in regard to irrigation and labour requirements are very similar to those in South China. Besides, no direct comparison is here attempted. The point to be observed is, rather, that under identical conditions of soil, climate, and irrigation, the cost of rice production in Japan rises so steeply per land unit with the diminishing size of the holding that any expected advantages from small-scale cultivation disappear. While the yield per land unit may be slightly higher for the smaller holding, the writer has been assured that the difference is inconsequential in comparison with the great disparity of production costs as between the holdings of less than five cho and those of more than five cho.

That land use on the larger scale is more advantageous than that on the smaller is also true in its bearing on the tax burden. It is even more apparent in regard to the so-called equipment expenses—such as house, implements, and land improvement. The peasant family with less than 5 tan has to allow Y 4.07 per tan as equipment expenses; but the peasant family with more than 5 cho (50 tan) needs only Y 1.80 for this purpose.

The statistics of the Japanese Imperial Agricultural Association further show that if a peasant family owning a holding of less than 3½ cho cultivates only rice, its income will not be sufficient to meet its annual expenditure. The minimum scale of rice cultivation yielding a profit they consider to be 3½ cho. Now, 1 tan is 9.6 are, or 0.245 acre, or 1.6 mow; and 3½ cho is equal to 56 mow. Apparently, many small peasants in Japan can maintain their families on this amount of land; but in reality they are receiving only part of what would be regarded as a "living wage" in the case of hired labourers. For, the earnings of the peasant cultivator are never fully realized. No one hands him a pay envelope or even a string of cash at the end of the week or of the harvest season. He never knows for certain whether his enterprise "pays" or not; and very often, as we have already seen, the size of the holding alone shows that he cannot possibly make enough to have anything left over when the family is fed and rent and taxes have been paid.

Let us assume that the peasant and his family are working for someone else and expend the same amount of labour on their employer's land which it would take to cultivate their own little holding of four tan. In that case, the Japanese investigator tells us, the family would earn Y 83.20. This sum may be regarded, then, as the "home labour wage" for a peasant family cultivating four tan. The rates have been worked out for different sizes of holdings, on the ground that with each increase in the size of the holding the labour power of the family is more fully utilized. Consequently, the equivalent for a hired family's wage which the employment of the family on its own holding ought to realize varies per tan with the size of that holding, as is roughly indicated in the following table:

Area of Holding	Would-be Earnings of Family per Tan According to Current Wage Rate
Below 5 tan	¥20.80
5 tan to 1 cho	21.90
2½ to 3 cho	22.05
Above 5 cho	23.51

According to the above table, the peasant family cultivating less than 3 cho should receive on the average between 20 and 22 yen per tan for its home labour. But this includes only what the land should yield the worker after all expenses have been paid. If we add the assessed cost of production for such a holding, namely between Y 60 and Y 70, we get a total of Y 80 to Y 92 which one tan must pay. If, however, we take a holding of five cho or more, the estimated value of the labour put into it by the family is Y 23.51 to which must be added Y 48.00 for other items of production cost, making a total of only Y 71.51 per tan. It will be seen, therefore, that the peasant is more likely to find his own labour and that of members of his family rewarded when the holding to which they apply their labour is 5 cho or more. Strictly speaking, therefore, the rational scale of rice cultivation to ensure a wage above bare subsistence should be 5 cho, the equivalent of 80 mow. In any case, the majority of the Japanese rice peasants do not receive an adequate remuneration for their labour. Mr. Aizo Sado has expressed this in his short essay, published in *Jikyoku Shimbun,* Tokyo, July 2, 1934, as follows: "The average cultivation area which is less than 1 cho per family is the paramount obstacle before the development of Japanese agriculture. . . . The misery and suffering in Japanese village life can hardly be ameliorated unless such a system of agriculture is changed."

E. F. Penrose, in his study of *Population Theories and Their Application With Special Reference to Japan* (Food Research Institute, Stanford University, 1934, p. 138), voices the same opinion when he says:

"The chemical and botanical and the commercial revolutions have been superimposed on a medieval and feudal social structure, and there has been no parallel revolution in the land system and in the size of the productive units in agriculture. . . . The size of the productive unit, however appropriate it may have been to an earlier technique, now limits the scope of the practicable measures of improvement. There is no room for doubt that a very large number of Japanese farms are far smaller than is economically desirable."

In the report of the mission of the Federation of British Industries which visited Manchuria in the autumn of 1934, a similar statement occurs with respect to the present land situation in that country:

"It is open to doubt whether the expenditure necessary for a greater mechanization of agriculture would prove profitable, unless the acreage of an individual farm were large enough to justify it. In case of the smaller farms, which are in the great majority, mechanization would not appear to be an economic possibility." (Appendix, Barnby Report, London, 1935).

To come back to China Proper, Wittfogel points out that the extreme parcellation which is to be found in most parts of the country today by no means corresponds to a requirement given by natural conditions but, on the contrary, has taken place in historical times—namely, beginning with the end of the Chou dynasty—of large-scale production under a village system of semi-communistic character. It took a thousand years, he finds, for the old forms of large-scale farming to give way to the familial type of farming with its minute sub-division of the land which we know today. (K. A. Wittfogel, *Wirtschaft und Gesellschaft Chinas,* Leipzig, 1931, p. 350). To claim that any particular size of farm unit represents the optimum from the point of view of production leaves out of account the social system which determines the effective use of labour. The uncritical assurance of many foreign writers that the small and even miniature holding is in keeping with a special genius of the Chinese people for small farming has created a myth which is confirmed neither by historical data nor by an adequate analysis of present-day conditions. (See *ibid.*, to p. 381.)

Most recent studies by agricultural experts indicate that in many parts of China the average size of farm unit is much too small for profitable use. Nor is this true only of one kind of crop or of one type of farm management or another. In Kwangtung, in spite of its favorable natural conditions, the situation in this regard is particularly bad. Here agriculture is not yielding any real remuneration to the cultivator himself, in most cases, except the barest subsistence; and not always that. For, the average size of holding in this province is even smaller than it is in Japan and in Manchuria, and the proportionate number of holdings of the very smallest size is greater. Among 840 peasant families, excluding the hired agricultural labourers, in the ten representative villages of Pan-yu, as many as 96 per cent cultivate less than 30 mow; and 30 mow is still below an area of 2 cho. (See table 14). Even though there are two crops annually in Kwangtung, the cultivation of 2 cho is certainly below the minimum area that can pay home labour the equivalent of an agricultural labourer's wage when all other expenses have been met. Such a petty scale of agriculture predominates in the entire province, especially in the three delta regions of Si-kang, Han-kang, and Lo-cheng-kang, as well as in the north-eastern portion of the island of Hainan. According to investigations carried out in 1932 by the Agricultural College of the present National Chung-shan University, four out of every five of the peasant families in Kao-yao cultivate between 5 to 20 mow; two out of every five of the peasant families in Sze-hwei cultivate less than 10 mow and one-half of them from 10 to 30 mow; one-half of the peasant families in K'ai-p'ing cultivate less than 10 mow per family, and less than one-third from 10 to 20 mow; also one-half of the peasant families in Hoh-p'u cultivate less than 10 mow per family, and two-fifths cultivate from 10 to 20 mow. In the other districts of Chih-k'i, T'ai-shan, Ling-shan, and Sin-hsing, 70 per cent of the peasant families have an average area of cultivation of less than 10 mow; and the districts of Kwangning and Kai-kien would probably represent an extreme case with 80 per cent of the peasant families in the former and 90 per cent of those in the latter cultivating less than 10 mow per family (see *General Survey of Agriculture in Kwangtung,* second part of second report, August, 1933, published by Chung-shan University).

These large differences in the predominant sizes of holdings are explained chiefly by differences in the degree of fertility and in the influence of the price of land. The latter is determined in many cases by overseas remittances, that is, the number of emigrants who have set forth from a given community and have done well abroad; in these cases, the price of land and therewith the size of holdings reflects a relative desire to invest, dependent upon the available free capital and other investment opportunities, rather than different degrees of value from the cultivator's point of view, and hardly at all such factors as nearness to towns and to means of transportation which are so influential on land prices and sizes of land holdings in Western countries.

Of course, the unsatisfied demand for land which may be read in such figures as those given above is not unrelated to the situation of ownership. Exactly how close this relationship is we shall now examine. As we have seen, there is a highly concentrated owner-ship and at the same time a widely distributed use of the land, with the result that nearly all of the holdings are uneconomically small In other words, one might speak of an incongruity between land owning and land using, between private ownership and common need: the cultivators have not enough land on which to live, and, as we shall presently see, most of the land is owned by those who do not cultivate. Wherever such a situation exists, it is the basic obstacle to the solution of the agrarian problem. As the Japanese investigation has shown, even small peasants who own their land can hardly bear all the necessary cost of production. It would be doubly difficult, therefore, for the tenants to make a living in a region where the holdings are as small as was shown above. Suppose we forget for the moment the poor peasants and consider only the middle and the rich peasants, an incongruous relation between ownership and utilization may be seen in the table on page 19.

It will be seen that in this district the middle peasants cultivate, on the average, more than three times as much land as they own, while the rich peasants cultivate only a little more than twice the area of the land they own.

AVERAGE AREA OF LAND OWNED AND CULTIVATED PER PERSON AMONG MIDDLE AND RICH PEASANTS*

(Ten Representative Villages in the District of Pan-yu, 1933)

Peasant Class	Land Possessed	Land Cultivated
Middle	0.73 mow	2.40 mow
Rich	1.75	3.95

* In the present instance, not families but individual "mouths to feed" are taken as the units of comparison. For detailed figures see tables 18 and 19.

The incongruity between farm holding and size of owned land area is even greater if we compare the proportions in this respect for the landlords with those for the peasant class as a whole. Of

PERCENTAGE OF CULTIVATED LAND AREA LEASED BY PEASANTS FROM RESIDENT PRIVATE LANDLORDS

(Ten Representative Villages in the District of Pan-yu, 1933)

Village	Total Área of Land Cultivated by Peasants	Total Area of Land Rented from Landlords	Percentage of Cultivated Area Leased from Landlords
Mei-tien	1,116.7	937.6	84.0
Nan-pu	1,393.4	1,117.9	80.2
Kang-sin	434.5	331.8	76.4
Sha-dien-kang	1,179.6	899.1	76.2
Ting-lung-fong	635.5	402.5	63.3
Pei-shan	1,070.3	659.8	61.6
Huang-pien	626.5	377.1	60.2
Kiu-tseng	1,065.9	588.7	55.2
Kwei-tien	206.5	81.7	39.6
Lung-tien	327.1	113.9	34.8
Total	8,056.0	5,510.1	(aver.)68.4

all the land cultivated by the peasants of Pan-yu, more than two-thirds (68.4 per cent) is rented from the local landlords. By this class are meant those who own land but do not cultivate any part of it other than perhaps a small garden or a patch of mulberry or fruit trees. In the present instance, only those landlords are counted who are individual or, more often, family owners and reside in the villages; and not clan and other collective or absentee owners.

The extent to which cultivated land has passed into the hands of local private landlords, as above defined, varies, as we see, from village to village. On the whole, the local differences in this respect seem to reflect differences in fertility. The land in these villages is mostly irrigated, and in the villages with richer soil wealth is more apt to become concentrated than it is in the villages where the natural conditions are poorer and where nearly all the cultivators make a poor living. For other possible explanations of these variations, see also page 18.

Five years before the facts were obtained on which are based the figures just given, the percentage of the land owned by these landlords in the total area of land cultivated by the peasants was 67.1; it has increased by 2 per cent within this short period. Of all the land under cultivation in Pan-yu, nearly three-quarters is rented (see table 7), but more than two-thirds is rented from the landlords, as here defined, and only 5 per cent from small merchants and other village families.

These landlords are, of course, only a small and local group of a much larger class. Generally speaking, the landlords choose to stay in towns and cities, and are out of the reach of any village survey. Among them are many merchants and returned emigrants. These latter are a special feature of the Kwangtung economy; some emigrants acquire considerable land property even while they are still overseas. Furthermore, the vast majority of the big landlords in Kwangtung are corporate landlords—such as the clan and the temple. The minority of landlords who reside in the villages and most of whom own comparatively little certainly do not represent the entire force of landlordism.

Now, apart from the non-residential landlords and the collective landlords, we also have village families which possess more land than the average middle peasant and rent out more than one-half of it; with the possible exception of those concubines whose status is that of an unpaid labourer, its members do not participate in field labour. A family under these three conditions is still considered as a peasant family when the major part of its income is not from rent, and when its rent income does not suffice to support it. Suppose, however, a family of this sort does get the major part of its income from rent and, in fact, is almost entirely supported by its rental income: to call this a peasant family is no longer quite realistic; and for present purposes we shall class it as a hyphenated peasant-landlord family with the landlord class. Incidentally it may be said that the number of such families is exceedingly small.

With these class definitions, we can now proceed to the following comparison:

LAND POSSESSION OF ALL TYPES OF VILLAGE FAMILIES
(Ten Representative Villages in Pan-yu District, 1933)

Families	Total Area of Land Owned	
	Mow	Per cent.
Landlord *	583.6	18.6
Peasant	2,442.3	77.6
Others	118.4	3.8
Total	3,144.3	100.0

* Excluding collective and non-residential, but including peasant-landlord families.

Although only one-fifth of the cultivated land area (19 per cent) is owned by the individual resident landlord families, their average land possession per family or per capita is much larger than that of the peasants. (See table on page 22).

The individual landlord families, constituting only 3 per cent of all the village families (see table 20), possess 19 per cent of the land and do not participate in agriculture. They are usually grain merchants, grocers, pawnbrokers, and individual money lenders, with a sprinkling also of retired civil and military petty officers. The extent to which they depend on land rents for a living varies a great deal. Furthermore, their land possession claims a larger proportion of fields of the better quality, whereas that of the peasant families has a larger proportion of poorer quality. Of the land owned by residential landlord families, three-fifths in

AVERAGE LAND POSSESSION PER FAMILY AND PER CAPITA
(Ten Representative Villages in the District of Pan-yu, 1933)

Families	Average per Family	Average per Capita
	Mow	Mow
Landlord *	16.7	3.83
Peasant	2.6	0.54
Others	0.5	0.13
Total	2.6	0.56

* Excluding collective and non-residential, including peasant-landlord families.

area is irrigated, and hence more fertile. Of the land owned by the peasant families, however, only one-half is irrigated. (See table 21).

We should pay special attention here to the fact that all statistics hitherto cited regarding the distribution of land ownership in Pan-yu do not include the so-called Sha-tien region. Literally, *sha* means sand, and *tien* means field. The vast delta region which has been formed by the sediments of the Pearl River is locally known as Sha-ku. *Ku* means region. Sha-ku is naturally the most fertile agricultural region in Kwangtung. All the fields in this Sha-ku are called Sha-tien. The largest number of such fertile fields is to be found in the district of Chung-shan; less in Pan-yu and in Shun-teh respectively; but there are sha-tien also in the districts of Tung-kwan, Pao-an, Sin-hwei, Nan-hai, and T'ai-shan. The total number of Sha-t'ien in Kwangtung is approximately 2,500,000 mow, which is one-sixteenth of all the cultivated land in the province. In this Sha-ku, a most fertile agricultural region, a surprisingly small proportion of the 85,000 peasant families possess any land. On more than 300,000 mow of the Sha-tien in Pan-yu, at least 40,000 peasants are labouring under a system of multiple sub-renting and extortionate rents in kind— amounting to from 70 to 80 per cent of the product. If we take this Sha-ku, the region practically without peasant owners, into the statistical account of land distribution in Pan-yu, then we see a very marked alteration in the previously cited percentages of cultivated land area owned by tenants and by landlords, and of the proportions of these classes in relation to the landless peasant families.

The extreme disparity of land distribution and the perpetual wretchedness of peasant life in this particular region, must have excited a certain emotionalism among many of the early party members of Kuomintang which, assisted by the Chinese Communists, started revolutionary activities in Kwangtung. About six years later, in 1931, a lingering echo of Dr. Sun Yat-sen, the founder of the Chinese Revolution, may still be traced in a preface to the Annual of the Land Bureau of Chung-shan. "The agrarian problem is fundamental to our national livelihood," begins this preface. "If this problem were to be rightly solved, naturally there would be a proper way out for our national livelihood. Only by the solution of this problem can mankind gradually get rid of war. Equality in land ownership has been the principle advocated by the Kuomintang. Our chief purpose is to prevent the monopoly by a few, and to provide equal rights and equal opportunity of land utilization for all the people." If it be true that the depth of human suffering gives birth to the highest aspirations, we may perhaps discern behind such lofty words a hideous reality.

CHAPTER II

THE ECONOMIC AND POLITICAL POSITION OF
THE COLLECTIVE LANDLORDS

WHEN THE land is owned actually or nominally by more than one individual family, and is directly or indirectly rented to the peasants for cultivation, its owner is generally called a collective landlord. Instead of being strictly individual, property right in China still dominantly belongs to the family. Thus, by a *private landlord,* we mean an individual family which has rented out its land, in contradistinction to the *collective landlord* by whom we mean a larger corporate body. The private landlords in Kwangtung have an influence, economically as well as politically, much inferior to that of the collective landlords. Different types of collective landlords, however, should be distinguished. Besides the lands owned by public bodies and charity organizations, the total extent of which does not claim a considerable proportion in the cultivated land area of Kwangtung, there are several other forms of collective ownership of land, such as the "education land", the temple land, land owned by certain social organizations or guilds of merchants, and the ancestral land not yet divided by the component families of a clan.

The income from the rents collected on the state land set aside for education is intended to defray the expenses of worshipping Confucius, of subsidizing poor scholars, and more recently of maintaining public schools. It is small in area and not so significant in Kwangtung as it is in some other provinces, such as Shantung or Yunnan. In Chun-shan, agriculturally the richest district of the province, the "education land" is not more than a one-thousandth part of the cultivated area. In another rich district, Ch'ao-an, only one out of every three hundred mow is devoted to education. Of course, there are some districts with comparatively more "education land"; in Ling-shan, it claims 1 per cent of the cultivated land; in Wung-yuen 2 per cent; in Ying-teh also 2 per cent; and in Hwei-yang 3 per cent. Perhaps Meu-ming has the highest percentage of "education land", which here occupies 5 per cent of the cultivated area. Through a continuous process of incorporation of temple lands and lands of merchant organizations, the so-called "education land" in Hoh-p'u is now nearly one-fifth of the cultivated land. But this was brought about by a political coup in a situation in which political and economic power were concentrated to an unusual degree, and no other district in Kwangtung has carried out this process to the same extent.

Neither does the temple land in Kwangtung play as important a role in the agrarian relations as it does in the Yangtze provinces. Only 3 out of every 1,000 mow cultivated in Chung-shan are temple land. In Ch'ao-an, 1 out of every 600 mow is of temple land. In the districts of Hwei-yang, Wung-yuen, and Meu-ming, the temple land occupies only 1 per cent of the cultivated area. Even in Ying-teh, one of the most mountaineous districts of the province, where one would expect to find a comparatively large number of temples, the total area of all the temple lands amounts to less than 4 per cent of the cultivated land.

The land belonging to social organizations of merchants is to be found mostly in the south-western part of Kwangtung. In the several districts of this part of the province, wealthy merchants many years ago, for their common worship of some god and for the purpose of providing for their common social amenities, established, under various names, societies of a religious and social nature. These societies, or *Hwei,* acquired land properties with funds made up of their membership fees and of free contributions. The land, in this case, is called *Hwei-tien.* Usually one Hwei is in the possession of 30 or 40, up to 150 or 160 mow. This land property, or Hwei-tien, is managed by an official elected from among the members of the Hwei. Occasionally this official is assisted by some of the members, especially when the collection of rents becomes a task of considerable magnitude. In the district of Meu-ming there used to be at one time several hundreds of such Hwei under various names; the most influential of them, which is still popular today, is called Si-tai Hwei. It is said that Si-tai was the name of a woman general in the T'ang Dynasty, during the ninth century, who defended the district against invaders. Long ago she has been deified, and her temple stands today in the city of Meu-ming. Theatrical performances still take place annually in front of her statue. Another very popular Hwei in southwestern Kwangtung is the so-called P'ien-shin Hwei, which is located in Lien-kiang. Its membership comprises several hundreds of families; the accumulation of its membership fees has been invested entirely in land purchase; and within the past fifteen years or so, its Hwei-tien has increased tenfold. The income of Pien-shin Hwei is being used in equal parts for three purposes: one-third of it is for maintaining a sort of religious worship, another third is for subsidizing school attendance among its members, and the last third is for financing a middle school in the city.

The founding of such Hwei as those described here has taken place mostly in the middle of the eighteenth century. The first two decades of the nineteenth century witnessed the establishment of only a few Hwei. In recent years no new ones have come into existence; and even the well-established ones have undergone a gradual but irresistible process of disintegration. The local governmental policy of confiscating some of the Hwei-tien and incorporating them into the "education land" of the district has no doubt accelerated this process. Forestalling the action of the local government, many of the Hwei have sold their land and divided the money among the member families. Thus the number of Hwei-tien has been decreasing year by year, till today it assumes a feeble position as collectively owned land. Less than 1 per cent of the cultivated land in Hwa-hsien remains as Hwei-tien. Less than 2 per cent of the cultivated land in Tien-peh and less than 3 per cent in Ling-shan respectively belong to the Hwei. The percentage of Hwei-tien in Lien-kiang to the total cultivated land area of that district is as high as 5 per cent; and even the highest proportion which is in Meu-ming does not exceed 11 per cent.

Clan land is the one single dominating form of land owned in common which accounts for the continuing influence of collective landlordism in Kwangtung. It has the popular name of *Tsi-tien* or *Ch'ang-tien*; and still more often it is called *Tai-kung-tien*. *Tsi* means worshipping, and *Tai-kung* means the ancestors. When it is called *Ch'eng-ch'ang-tien,* as it is in some districts, it simply means the land for maintaining ancestral worship, which is performed twice a year in the clan temple. The ceremony in autumn is *Cheng* and that in winter is *Chang*. In the local chronicle of Mei-hsien, written about a hundred years ago, we find the following interesting passages:

"Not only the big clans possess Chen-chang-tien, but also the small ones and the sub-clans of a large one."

"It has been a long and well established tradition to maintain Tai-tien or the clan land for ancestral worship. The annual income thereof, besides defraying the expenditure for worship, has a threefold use. Those families sending their boys to the ancestral temple to study may receive a regular stipend; also scholars in the clan who have been admitted to the public ceremony of worshipping Confucius may receive an annual subsidy; and those scholars who are to participate in the civil service examinations either in the provincial or in the national capital, may have their traveling expenses partially or entirely paid from the clan fund."

"The finance of the clan does not confine itself to education. All the elders who are above sixty years of age receive an annual grant of rice and, on every occasion of ancestral worship, a certain amount of meat. Some of the very poor or permanently disabled members of the clan also enjoy such an annual grant. Some financial assistance is given, too, to those clan members who cannot meet the expense of their wedding or funeral. Whenever a severe famine occurs, relief is offered from the clan treasury."

In a revised edition of this Mei-hsien chronicle, published several decades later, emphasis is laid on the fact that the system of clan land is more or less the same throughout the province; and this system is praised as an excellent traditional way of providing for social work and charity.

Another district chronicle, that of Kwang-ning, published in 1824, contains the following precise statement:

"The wealthy families take particular trouble to erect clan temples and to institute clan lands. The latter are for the maintenance of the former, and no matter how poor the clan may become, no clan land may be disposed of privately."

That the clan land may not be privately sold is indeed a world-wide decree—among American Indians, for example, and among the ancient Inca. A remarkable case of the seriousness with which the ancients have tried to impress it upon their descendants is to be found in one of the villages in the delta region of the Yangtze. Here, deeds of the clan land are kept not in paper form, but were from the beginning carved on stone tablets. These tablets were then set into the walls of the clan temple, so that clan members can hardly divide the land among themselves without a grievous offence against their religion, nor can easily effect the sale of that land. The deeds of the clan land in Kwangtung are not generally kept in such a strict form; nevertheless, this land is not subject to sale, unless by the common consent of all the clan elders. Early in the spring of 1934, the official of a certain Liu Clan in T'ai-shan, to whose hands the management of clan land had been entrusted, made a secret attempt to sell it. This was detected by his fellow members of the clan, and a general meeting was summoned to punish him. To atone for his guilt he was condemned to furnish pigs to offer a special sacrifice to the clan ancestors. Just because of this traditional difficulty of selling the clan land, together with the annual accumulation of rent which helps to enlarge the original estate, clan land or the so-called Tai-kung-tien provides collective landlordism with a firm basis.

Those who have much can easily get more; and those who have little can easily lose more; this may not be the will of God, but up to the present it seems to be the will of men. This also is the way of the expansion of clan lands, especially in the Sha-ku, the fertile delta region of the Pearl River. Local chronicles as well as individual writings have frequently recorded incidents which relate how big land fortunes have been acquired by powerful clans. River current and sea tide work daily and incessantly to bring sediments and to form sandy but exceedingly fertile lands; and by protection and the planting of a certain kind of grass thereon, they may be converted into cultivable fields within three years. For such new lands, the wealthy clans compete among themselves to pay the taxes, in order that they might claim their ownership. Adjacent strips of land already under cultivation and belonging to families of rather feeble standing, are often simultaneously taken by encroachment, subsequently upheld by the local courts; thus the big and powerful clans incorporate in their possessions not only the cultivable but also the cultivated. Should the losing families attempt to resist, their harvests are seized by the aggressive clans which often use brutal force in the certainty that in case of litigation their unjust claims would be upheld. The history of the Pearl River Delta has carried with it many a sanguinary harvest-capture. Violent disputes between clans over the Sha-tien, similar to those over irrigation in the mountaineous regions between upland and lowland peasants and their clans, give birth to clan wars on a considerable scale. It has become a habit with the wealthy clans to hire mercenary fighters outside their own membership. This is nothing new in Chinese history; but even in recent times provincial and local governments have not yet succeeded in holding it in check. Events of this sort must have so strongly impressed the minds of many men of letters that in the literature of Chung-shan, written about sixty years ago, frequent reference is made to the fact that, in spite of the governmental policy, in opening up land for primary cultivation to give it to the poor, wealthy clans actually usurp it in the name of individual claimants; and that even after boundary lines have been marked, the more powerful clans encroach upon the weaker and simply change the boundary marks, though not always without violence.

The farming method in Sha-ku contributes also towards the augmentation of clan land or Tai-kung-tien ("ancestral fields"), for more extensive agriculture is practised here than in other rice regions. This method is locally known as *Tsan-kao*; *tsan* means inserting and *kao* is simply a synonym for rice-plant. By the process of Tsan-kao, the seedlings of a second crop are planted in between the rows at most twenty days after the planting of those of the first crop. Of course, the second seedlings grow to maturity only after the harvest of the first crop; but there is no need for a second ploughing. The production by Tsan-kao not only means labour saving, but also needs no additional fertilizer. To compare, however, with the system of planting one crop after harvesting the other, that is, two entirely separate plantings a year, which is the common practice elsewhere, Tsan-kao inevitably yields from 20 to 30 per cent less.

The primary reason for this unorthodoxy in farming method is that the new land of the Sha-ku was richer, so that two crops could be secured without complete re-plowing. But this original richness of the soil is rapidly disappearing because the taking of two crops without a second plowing and without adequate fertilizing practically amounts to what in the West is called "mining" the land. The actual cause of this devastating and seemingly irrational process is here, as so often in such cases, the exploitation of the peasants by an excessive rent charge. That is, rents increase and make for a more and more frantic effort to extract wealth from the soil while the fertility of the land is diminishing. Thus crops gradually decrease and necessitate a larger area of cultivation to support the producers.

In the most fertile portion of the Pearl River Delta, it requires from 60 to 70 mow of Sha-tien to support a tenant family of the lowest standard of living. In other words, the minimum size of a farm holding must in practice be bigger in Sha-ku than in other parts of Kwangtung. And this accounts for the unwillingness on the part of the Sha-ku tenants to cultivate an area of less than 60 or 70 mow. Then, because of the extremely poor condition of communications, their landlords, that is, usually the clan and family elders, hardly ever visit the Sha-ku personally, and the land has never been properly surveyed, so that no one knows exactly where the field boundaries are, although the boundaries between clan properties, as we have seen, are quite well established and carefully guarded. This accounts for the unwillingness on the part of the Sha-ku clans to divide the land among their members: they would rather divide the income from the rent, whenever a division of family property occurs. Sometimes the income from the rent is distributed among the member families according to the number of individuals, and sometimes according to the number of sub-families. In Pan-yu both methods are in use: the clans in the village of Sha-wan adopt the former, and those in the village of Nan-tseng adopt the latter. When the undivided land of the family is handed down to the succeeding generation, it is as a matter of course re-absorbed by the main body of the clan estate or Tai-kung-tien. This custom of dividing rent instead of land considerably helps to increase the amount of the clan land because each family adds to its own land possession from time to time. This procedure may seem peculiar to Western minds, since naturally one would expect the elders of a

There are comparatively less extensive clan lands in the southwestern part of Kwangtung. This can be seen from the following figures.

PROPORTION OF CLAN LAND IN THE CULTIVATED AREA
(Twenty Districts of the Southwestern Part of Kwangtung)

District	Per Cent.	District	Per Cent.	District	Per Cent.
Hwa-hsien	20	Ting-an	20	Yang-kiang	40
Wen-chang	20	Meu-ming	30	Yang-ch'un	40
Hoh-pu	10	Sin-i	45	Sui-k'i	10
Wu-chwan	25	Ling-shui	10	T'ien-peh	35
Lien-kiang	25	Tan-hsien	5	Loh-hwei	20
Ling-shan	20	K'iung-shan	15	K'iung-tung	15
Lo-ting	40	Ch'eng-mai	15		

In the districts of the North River Valley, the percentage of clan land also is not very high:

PROPORTION OF CLAN LAND IN THE CULTIVATED AREA
(Eleven Districts of the Northern Part of Kwangtung)

District	Per Cent.	District	Per Cent.	District	Per Cent.
Jen-nwa	20	Ying-teh	20	Wung-yuen	12
Kuh-kiang	10	Ju-yuen	40	Tsing-yuen	15
Fuh-kang	10	Nan-hsiung	20	Loh-chang	30
Hwa-hsien	50	Lien-hsien	50		

Perhaps Lien-hsien and Hwa-hsien must be regarded as unusual places in the valley of the North River; the percentage of the clan land is as high here as in Pan-yu and Hwei-yang. According to the statistics for 17 villages of Hwa-hsien, there are 39,050 mow of cultivated land; of these 49.3 per cent are clan lands, 0.1 per cent temple lands, 1.5 per cent other collectively owned lands, and the remaining 49.1 per cent lands belonging to private families.

In the valley of Han River, and also in that of the East River, the percentage of clan land is usually high, as may be seen from the following table.

PROPORTION OF CLAN LAND TO CULTIVATED AREA
(Seventeen Districts of the Eastern Part of Kwangtung)

District	Per Cent.	District	Per Cent.	District	Per Cent.
Tung-kwan	20	Hai-fung	40	Ho-yuen	30
Hwei-yang	50	Tsz-kin	40	Hwo-ping	20
Pan-yu	50	Poh-lo	40	Ping-yuen	40
Hsing-ning	25	Pao-an	30	Wu-hwa	30
Mei-hsien	40	Chiao-ling	40	Chao-an	30
Lung-chw'an	25	Hwei-lai	40		

The highest percentage of clan land occurs among the districts of the West River, or even oftener in the delta of the Pearl River, where most of the new land made by sea and river, the Sha-ku, is to be found. In many of these districts 40 per cent or more of the cultivated land belong to the clans.

PROPORTION OF CLAN LAND TO CULTIVATED AREA
(Fifteen Districts of the Middle-South Part of Kwangtung)

District	Per Cent.	District	Per Cent.	District	Per Cent.
Chung-shan	50	Kao-yao	40	Teh-k'ing	40
Tai-shan	50	Kwang-ning	10	Yun-fou	30
Sze-hwei	30	Yuh-nan	40	En-p'ing	40
Nan-hai	40	Hoh-shan	40	K'ai-p'ing	40
Shun-teh	60	Sin-hwei	60	Sin-hsing	30

Of all the districts cited above, 17 have been directly investigated. They are Chung-shan, Tai-shan, Kao-yao, Shun-teh, Kwang-ning, Mei-hsien, Hwei-yang, Pan-yu, Chao-an, Kuh-kiang, Ying-teh, Wung-yuen, Loh-chang, Meu-ming, Lien-kiang, Hoh-pu, and Ling-shan. The percentages of clan lands of the other 46 districts have been obtained through correspondence from 294 villages. Of these 63 districts, 20 are located in the southwestern part of the province, 17 in the east, 15 in the middle-south, and 11 in the north. Generally speaking, 23 per cent of the cultivated area in the southwestern part of Kwangtung, 25 per cent in the north, 35 per cent in the east, and 40 per cent in the middle-south, are clan lands. On the delta of the Pearl River, one-half of the cultivated land is clan land. Indeed, we can safely say that one-third of the cultivated land of the entire province is clan land. Based upon the lowest estimate, there are a little over 42,000,000 mow of cultivated land in Kwangtung; and no less than 35 per cent of this area owned by clans and other kinds of corporate bodies. Furthermore, 60 per cent of the cultivated land is being irrigated; and among the irrigated lands, the percentage of collective lands is even higher. Even if we reckon with 35 per cent, and figure on an average rent of 10 Yuan per mow, then some 14,700,000 mow of such collective lands in Kwangtung must yield a total rent of 147,000,000 Yuan every year, of which the clans alone collect 126,000,000.

Between 1928 and 1930 the average annual land tax of the whole province was about 5,400,000 Yuan, of which 1,400,000 Yuan was collected from the fertile Sha-ku. To quote the *Statistical Monograph* (Vol. 2, page 29), edited by the Secretariat of the Kwangtung Provincial Government, "This province is one of the richest in the whole country; with the exception of Kiang-su, no province can compete with it in wealth. The combined income of both provincial and national revenues amounts to 70,000,000 Yuan every year." The importance of the rents collected on the clan and other collective lands of Kwangtung may, therefore, roughly be described as representing about one-third of the land rents of the whole province, almost thirty times the revenue from the annual land tax, and more than twice the total amount collected by all taxes together.

In theory, of course, the rents drawn from the land by corporate ownership revert to the benefit of the peasants themselves, on the assumption that most of them belong to a clan in their village and thus are part owners. Actually, however, the situation may be compared with that of the public utilities in the United States, with their widespread nominal ownership but concentration of control and profits in a few hands. Only, the position of the Kwangtung peasant is far worse than that of the corresponding American householder; for he not only has to pay a monopoly price for a service controlled by a corporate body, but is dependent on that monopoly for an essential means of livelihood.

The peasants in Kwangtung are concerned, however, with clan economy not only because of the rent they have to pay for the use of its land, but also because of the interest they have to pay on clan loans. In the northern and southwestern parts of the province, many tenants take loans from clans in grain as well as in cash. Some use the loan as a part of their means of production, some even use the loan to pay their rent. In the 4th sub-district of Meu-ming, for instance, 5 per cent of all the peasants are cash borrowers, and have to pay an annual interest of from 30 to 50 per cent. No less than 80 per cent of the rent income of the various clans in Hwahsien, near Canton, is loaned to the peasants, to earn a monthly interest of 1½ or 2 per cent.

At this rate, the indebtedness of the peasants to the clans of that district would appear to be growing at the rate of about 20 per cent a year. If the debts were repaid in a year, the funds of the clans would grow so rapidly that only further large land purchases or a drastic lowering of the interest rates could keep these funds employed. But actually the process is made possible by a constant leakage of clan funds through the extension of financial privileges to the few families which are actually in control. Another reason is, of course, that only a very small part of the peasant loans are repaid; it is possible for the clans to continue charging high and, as we shall see below, even usurious interest rates because the peasants constantly have to make new loans to pay their old debts.

Within one year both the principal and the interest are supposed to be paid, at least the interest is supposed to be duly discharged. All overdue interest is counted as a part of the principal, to bear further interest. When the unpaid interest equals the principal, the property of the indebted peasant is inevitably taken away; and in case this seized property does not suffice to pay his debt, it is often supplemented by the property of his nearest relatives. Under customary law in this part of Kwangtung, a creditor has the right to go beyond the individual debtor to his nearest blood relation for satisfaction of his debt and, if unsuccessful in that quarter, to follow his claim through different degrees of relationship, if necessary to the leaders of the clan itself.

In fact, rent and indebtedness have a very close connection. Take, for instance, a big village, Sin-lung-hsiang, in the district of Shun-teh, where 40 per cent of the cultivated land belongs to the clans: the tenants here pay their rent in spring and autumn; but monthly interest must be paid on the rent overdue. One-half of the entire delta of the Pearl River is clan land, and in a great majority of cases, its rent is being paid in advance of the harvest. This practice leads straight to usury.

To understand the economic influence of the clan we must now direct our attention to its social composition, its organization, and its functioning. In Kwangtung, four out of every five peasants, or more, live with their clans. Usually one village is inhabited by one clan. Even if there is more than one clan, each clan occupies a distinct section of the village; there is hardly a mixed neighborhood. In Chao-an, for instance, nearly one-half of the villages of the entire district are inhabited by people bearing the same clan name. More than one-half of the villages of Hwei-yang are so inhabited. Each clan or sub-clan has its own clan land under various names, denoting the origin of the property, such as the "primary" clan land, the "fifth generation" clan land, the "seventh generation" clan land, the "second sub-clan" land, the "third sub-clan" land, etc. The traditional indivisibility of the clan land is the explanation why for so many generations the members live together in the same place and even those who have long lived abroad continue to look upon it as their home.

Then, each clan or sub-clan has its own officers, by different names—such as the clan head, the clan chief, the clan trustee, the clan manager, the clan treasurer, the clan chief-accountant, and so forth. As a rule, the clan head is the oldest man of the clan, and the clan chief or clan trustee is selected from among the oldest generation living. Heads, chiefs, and trustees hold merely honorary positions in the clan; the clan managers, the clan treasurers, and the clan chief-accountants are the ones who exercise real power. Men of real power are elected to their offices sometimes by the clan elders beyond 50 or 60 years of age, sometimes by the various sub-clans, and even more often by clan members at large on the occasion of their common ancestral worship. As a matter of fact, they are always from the so-called strong branches of the clan, that is, those composed of the largest number of families and individuals. And they themselves are supposed to be "rich and reliable", "learned and rational." Often when the "rich and reliable" consider themselves not quite "learned and rational" enough, they recommend somebody else to be appointed in their place. Thus the clan manager, the clan treasurer, or the clan chief-accountant is usually somebody who in his early years has passed the civil service examination, or somebody who has graduated from a certain provincial school, or even more often some retired bureaucrat who commands a rather ill-defined prestige in the locality. The "rich and reliable", however, always has the last word to say in matters of clan finance. Nominally, the clan treasurer or the clan chief-accountant holds his office for one year, but he may be re-appointed year after year. The tenure of this office in Ying-teh is from three to five years. In other districts it is often an appointment for life. In most of the cases in T'ai-shan, it is even hereditary.

All the incomes of the clan—consisting mostly of fish pond rent, house rent, land rent, and interest on clan loans—come under the management and control of the clan treasurer or the accountant. After defraying taxes, temple expenditures, cost of repair on clan properties, and the various subsidies to clan members for education, all clan incomes are left to his custody. Through the very process of his selection he has a position of such power that he can always handle this fund in his own interest without having to fear opposition. Too many clan treasurers never publish a detailed account. Often some of the rent from clan land is used to pay the land tax of the private families in control of the clan finances. Thus, notwithstanding that the clan land cannot be freely disposed of, the clan income is in reality at the free disposal of the clan officer. The common property of a clan is so manipulated as to become a modified form of private property. The vast sum of clan incomes, representing the fruit of the labour of the multitudes, is quietly passing into the possession of a relatively few people.

The history of this decline of the clans remains yet to be written. It must suffice here to indicate some of the main causes. These are linked up, of course, with the larger forces that have impinged upon the traditional social structure of China. Whether these be envisaged primarily as domestic or as foreign, as the collapse of an individualistic economy which has outlived its usefulness or as "the hammer of Western capitalism", the first concrete symptom was an increase in luxury. And luxury means demand for more commodities, many of them imported. Artificially fostered to permit the country's exploitation, this demand produces an ever growing substitution of money payments for payments in kind, and with the substitution also of an ever steeper rise of rent and interest rates and taxes.

In the rural community this trend has made for a substitution of cash crops for subsistence crops and, with the consequent increase of commercial crops, an intensification of the class division in village society. This has taken the form, in the main, of the creation of a new exploiting class which is able to turn the common heritage, such as the clan lands, to individual uses and, on the other hand, a peasant tenant class without status and eventually bereft even of the ability to question the actions of those who exercise power. Once a member of a self-governing corporation and taking part in those of its decisions which affected his own fortunes, the peasant has become a mere cog in a machine in the running of which he has no say and the performance of which he often does not understand. In this general situation, the decline of the clan may be regarded as the outstanding symptom of a social disintegration to which all the ancient institutions must in turn succumb.

This process until recently has been a gradual one; and so far as the changing nature of the clan and of its control is concerned, it is as yet largely under cover. The great majority of the peasant members are ignorant of what is taking place behind the doors where clan officials confer with politicians and with business men. Those of the more prosperous peasants who do not belong to the favoured families often are indignant over some experience of "squeeze" or injustice but helpless, since those who control the clan funds also control all possible means of legal redress. No one knows how far back extends the history of the alienation of clan assets which is the principal theme of the present chapter. But well informed persons consulted in connection with this study are agreed that things have become far worse in this respect in the last ten or fifteen years.

Furthermore, when the clans maintain their aggregate residence, the influence of the clan officers does not limit itself to financial matters. The clan officers are called upon to settle disputes within the clan and to punish those who commit offences against the clan. In a village named Huang-tang, in the district of Wung-yuen, two hundred families of the Huang clan may be regarded as an example of the judicial functioning of a clan. On the walls of the Huang ancestral temple are posted numerous proclamations from the clan authorities. One of these, dated July 9, 1933, reads as follows:

> "Anybody who steals taro, beans, or rice, may be arrested. If the thief is a member of the Huang clan, the person who effects the arrest should be given 2,000 cash; if the thief is not of the clan, the reward is 500 cash. To anyone who captures a thief of millet or peanuts, regardless of the status of the thief, a reward of 240 cash should be given."

On October 15th, of the same year, another clan proclamation of an administrative nature was made, regarding grass cutting in the hills belonging to the Huang clan:

> "Three days, the 19th, the 20th, and the 21st of each month, are now fixed for grass cutting. Six piculs per day are allowed to each family. For every 18 piculs, 7 cents, or about 180 cash, are to be levied. Nobody is permitted to go into the hills before the 19th, and any family which has overdue an interest payment on a clan loan is not at all admitted to the grass cutting."

The clan officer not only handles the tax on clan land, but also collects for the provincial government the land taxes of the private families in his clan. It is not unusual, therefore, that the clan officer himself acts as the chief tax collector for the whole village. He is supposed to distribute the official tax receipts to the various private families. In recent years, taxation has been increased, and taxes are often collected in advance; thus the clan officer who is at the same time an officer of the government undoubtedly has his political status further strengthened.

In the present system of rural self-government, the chiefs of sub-districts and the chiefs of villages, as well as their subordinates, are for the most part recommended by the authorities of powerful clans. Many of the clan officers themselves have become such chiefs concurrently. In theory the system may seem an embodiment of local autonomy admirably blending old Chinese institutions with Western principles of democracy. But actually it only means a further gain of power by those who already dominate the economic life of the community. In fact, economic and political controls are rapidly becoming merged; and neither the functions of the trustee of clan funds nor those of the administrative official stand out clearly today in many of these villages. In this twilight of responsibilities, many chances for graft and exploitation of the weak make their shameless appearance, evils for which there is no remedy in the system itself. Sometimes, the political posts become so satisfactory to these clan officials that they gradually drop their official titles in the clan. Just to illustrate, one village in Chao-an, two miles from a trading centre is inhabited by seven hundred people all of the same clan; their officers who are supposed to manage forty or more ancestral temples in the village and to take care of all the clan lands are no longer called the clan manager, the clan treasurer, or the clan chief-accountant, but are solely known by their new administrative titles. This set of officers, now equipped with additional political power, are in a position to enjoy most the properties originally instituted to worship their own forefathers.

It might be contended that such a strengthening of the clan managers is just what the fathers would have wished to see, that, indeed, it represents the fulfilment of an ancient dream of patriarchal rule. But actually these elders who are intriguing with others who exercise political and economic power are not strengthening the clan. Even where they do not deliberately line their own pockets, as so many of them do, they permit the clan to lose in inner cohesion, in social usefulness, and in prestige, while their own status in society rises to heights which the forefathers could hardly have imagined. They have assumed all the honours previously reserved for the dead: they have virtually made themselves over into "living ancestors."

CHAPTER III

THE SYSTEM OF TENANCY

THE LAND hunger in Kwangtung has compelled the peasants to resort to all sorts of measures to rent a few mow so that they might live. Since, as we have seen, the clans control a large part of the leased land, we will first direct our attention to the methods under which clan land is being leased, and later compare with this the methods under which private land is being leased.

The authorities who manage the clan land are naturally very keen to turn the existing land hunger to their own advantage. In Hwa-hsien and Meu-ming, for example, it has become customary for the tenants to offer some kind of bribery to the clan officer in order to get a chance of a successful bid for clan land. In Wung-yuen, the tenants must invite the clan officer to a feast, when the land lease is drawn. In the Lung-shan village of Shun-teh, a cash payment has come to be substituted for this form of bribery which at least had the merit of being sanctioned by custom; in this form it is explicitly known as "black money." A clan member may sometimes claim a prior right to use the land owned by his own clan; and sometimes, as in Wung-yuen, he may even pay a rent 20 per cent less than that paid by an outside tenant. But in most of the districts no such priority is recognized nor any rent reduction granted.

There are five ways of leasing out the clan land: (1) by apportioning it among all the applicants; (2) by leasing it to these in turn; (3) by leasing it out in one contract to some one person; (4) by using separate written contracts with a number of people; and (5) by making separate oral agreements with more than one tenant. The first two methods are practised within one and same clan; the other three have no regard to clan membership. While both the third and the fourth way require a written contract, the third way of renting out the land in a lump sets up a time limit by which the lease contract must be concluded. Under the system of leasing by contract, be it separate or in a lump, be it written or oral, should the tenant fail to pay his rent, or should be pay less than the specified sum, the authority who manages the clan estate may cancel the lease. When the lease is made only to clan members, in turn or in equal portions, the tenant also is forced to discontinue his cultivation in case of rent default. In Meu-ming, for instance, if the rent is not fully paid by the time of the spring ancestral worship, the tenant forfeits his use of clan land. In Sin-i, the rent payment may be deferred for only one year. In some districts, the tenant whose rent is in default is deprived of his share of meat at the celebration of ancestral worship, though he may still be allowed to continue his cultivation.

When the clan land is thrown open to the use of all clan members, the method seems to be a simple one. In a village called Lou-kang-fong, in the district of Sin-hwei, where 70 per cent of the land belongs to the clans, any clan member may apply for the lease of clan land, and no rent deposit is ever required. In another village, called Sha-chwan-ta-pien, in the district of Tai-shan, the entire population of some 130 families organize themselves into groups to apply for the lease of clan land; some have a tenure of three years and others of five years; the rent is paid twice a year, and in years of bad harvest it is always somewhat reduced. Often when a clan has comparatively little land, this is leased in turn to clan members. Such is the practice in many of the villages of Meu-ming, Loh-chang, Chiao-ling, Hwei-yang, Mei-hsien and Kiung-tung. This land lease in turn or by rotation is usually for one year and often does not require any rent deposit. In some places of Mei-hsien, the family which takes its turn to cultivate clan land pays a very moderate sum on deposit; but instead of paying a regular rent, it is held responsible to defray the expenditure of the clan's ancestral worship that year.

When the clan land is leased in a single lot, this is always announced beforehand to secure the best bid. Such announcements are usually made twice a year in the 1st and the 11th months of the lunar calendar, as in Hoh-shan, or in the 2nd and the 8th months, as in Kai-ping and En-ping. In some districts, however, only one time of the year is set up for the bids. This is so in the districts of Chao-an, Loh-chang, Fuh-kang, Ying-teh, and Pan-yu. The bids for the lease are usually taken in the autumn, and the rent is received the next spring, as is the custom in Chung-shan. Sometimes, in Shun-teh and in Sin-hwei, for instance, the rent payment is made twice a year. Regardless of whether it is due in one or two instalments, the rent is paid before the harvest; it is, indeed, a rent paid in advance of that gain which is making its payment possible.

With other forms of leasing also the clan land and the so-called "education land" in Kwangtung as a rule demand such a rent. The committee in charge of "education land" in Chung-shan has published the following official note in the local newspapers:

"The attention of our tenants is hereby called to the fact that the rent for 1934 should be paid by them on or before January 5th, 1934. Those whose rent is in default after this date forfeit all the rent deposit and whatever rent is already paid, and their cultivated land may be given to some new tenant."

In Chung-shan the rent deposit for clan land and also for "education land" is usually 20 per cent of the annual rent. A deposit for clan land is also required in the district of Shun-teh; and in Meu-ming and in Yun-fou, where this deposit is sometimes not necessary, a certain guarantor must be secured, instead.

When clan land is leased under separate written contracts to various tenants, a rent deposit may or may not be demanded. In some places of Sin-i and Meu-ming, where clan land is leased by separate written contracts, neither a deposit nor a guarantor is asked for. In the districts of Tai-shan and Chung-shan, however, a deposit, often amounting to more than one-half of the rent, is required. On the delta of the Pearl River, where rent in advance is generally prevailing, tenants have to deliver the rent at the clan temple. But in places where rent in grain is customary, such as in the districts of Jen-hwa, Lung-chwan, Wu-hwa, Ju-yuen, Nan-hsiung, etc., the manager or the treasurer of the clan often goes to the tenants for rent collection.

The practice of leasing clan land by oral agreement is decreasing. This tendency is particularly clear in Wung-yuen. Twenty-five years ago, nine-tenths of the clan lands in this district were leased out under oral contracts, but during the past ten years written contracts have become so prevalent that today less than one-tenth of clan lands are under oral lease contracts. In many other districts of Kwangtung, the lease of clan land by oral agreement is still very common, even in the district of Chao-an on the delta of the Han River where commerce is so well developed.

When the land of private families is leased, this is done either by written contract or by oral agreement. The latter method is applied mostly when the tenant is a relative or a close friend of the landlord. It is often used also when the tenure is very short, or when the tenant lives very near to the landlord. In such cases, a rent deposit is often not required. In a village called Ku-liu-pu, in Meu-ming, where 80 per cent of the cultivated land is clan land, private land is leased by oral agreement, while clan land is leased by written contract. Here no condition of rent deposit is attached to the contract; the rent itself is 60 per cent of the produce, regardless of the condition of the soil or the nature of the contract. More often, however, the oral agreement includes the condition of a rent deposit. In Chao-an this deposit amounts to from 10 to 50 per cent of the annual rent; in Chung-shan, though it is only 25 per cent, the tenant has to bring a burdensome present to the landlord at the time of the lease. In the village of Fou-shih, in Tai-shan, the deposit is as much as 50 or 60 per cent of the annual rent; and in some villages of Wu-hwa, this percentage runs up to 80. In Ling-shan, the rent deposit equals the rent itself; in this district the rent deposit has increased by 80 per cent within the past five years. In case of rent default, the landlord may return the deposit and lease the land to a new tenant. And if the landlord decides to take back the land and to cultivate it himself, the tenant has to give it up, no matter how punctually he has paid the rent.

Under the written contract system, private lands are usually leased with a rent deposit. There are many places, however, where a deposit is not demanded, such as Kuh-kiang, Ping-yuen, Yang-chun, Hwei-yang, and Wu-hwa. In Mei-hsien, where the written contract is mostly for five years and also subject to continuous renewal, rent deposit is rarely made. In Nan-hsiung, too, there is often no rent deposit; but in this case the landlord is entertained by the tenant right after the harvest. Where the landlord collects his rent twice a year, as in Ying-teh, the tenant has to entertain him or the agent accordingly. For a poor tenant family such entertainments are a heavy burden for which it may even have to go into debt. Again, when the tenant has to send the rent to his landlord, he has to take chickens to him every time, just because no rent deposit has been provided for. In a number of villages of Meu-ming, where private lands are leased without any deposit, the tenant has to agree beforehand to furnish some labour power if required to do so by his landlord. In Yang-shan, 10 cents per mow are given to the landlord instead of a rent deposit; and a piece of pork, remaining symbol of what once was a feast, provides the substitute, in case the land rented is smaller than one mow. Though no rent deposit is specified in the written contracts found in Loh-chang, the tenant here also must present, according to the local custom, some pork and cake to his landlord, at the time the lease is signed.

In the large majority of cases, the leases of private families require a definite rent deposit. This deposit has assumed various names in different localities. It is interesting that in the village of Chan-kang, in the northeastern corner of Pan-yu, the rent deposit is called "a fee for the feast"; evidently this money deposit has taken the place of the expenditure incurred in entertaining the landlord. The amount of money deposit also varies with different localities, ranging from 10 to 90 per cent of the annual rent. Usually a high deposit means a slightly lower rent. In the village of Tien-ya, Meu-ming, it is 20 per cent of the rent; in the villages of Chung-shan, it is from 20 to 70 per cent; in the village of Na-chien, Hwa-hsien, it is 90 per cent. Many places of Ju-yuen district have a rent deposit equivalent to the expected value of the year's rent which is paid in grain. In the southwestern part of Kwangtung, where the system of tenancy is still least affected by modern capitalism, the tenant has to bear other extra burdens besides that imposed upon him by having to pay so large a part of his rent in advance. By way of illustration, we may mention a few specific cases. In Kin-chu-tang, Sin-i, in addition to making a money deposit, the tenant has to work without pay for his landlord several days every year. In Li-tseng, Wu-chwan, the tenant has to offer his landlord pork and chicken, besides making the money deposit. In Han-tien-seng, Meu-ming, instead of pork, a regular gift of glutinous rice is made—sometimes of quite considerable quantity. In many villages of Tien-peh, and also of Lin-kao (on Hainan Island), additional to the rent deposit, both labour and gifts must be delivered to the landlord.

An unusual tenancy arrangement exists in the Sha-ku, where the fields are most fertile. Rich merchants and powerful gentry here rent in the land *en bloc,* chiefly from the clans, sometimes as much as several thousands or tens of thousands of mow. They themselves never cultivate or manage the estate, though they may enclose it against tide or bandits; they become a sort of second landlord or estate company, leasing out the land in separate holdings, sometimes directly to the cultivators, but more frequently to a series of third landlords, a system similar to that which prevails over large parts of India.

The second lessee or third landlord usually leases only one kind of land, either suitable for rice paddies or suitable for growing sugar cane—of which there are two varieties, usually kept apart, namely cane for direct consumption and cane of a higher sugar content which is sold to the crushing mills. Where he does not subdivide the land he has leased, his gain comes from sub-letting at a higher rent than he himself has to pay, a rent which he can exact by virtue of his greater experience as a rent collector or simply of his greater shrewdness and ruthlessness. Where he does subdivide, he is of course able to charge a higher rent also because the land hunger constantly forces the actual cultivators of the soil to pay more and more for less and less.

This second lessee does not, however, always have sub-tenants but may employ labour himself to grow sugar cane under a form of contract which in some respects resembles a lease. The labourers work from the first month till the middle of the ninth month of the lunar calendar, and are held responsible for all the field work except the cutting of canes for which day labourers are hired. They usually work two by two, father and son, two brothers, or husband and wife; two persons can together cultivate 6 mow of sugar cane for direct consumption or 15 mow of sugar cane for the mill. Where the wages are relatively high, 8 Yuan is that paid for cultivating one mow. Where they are the lowest, only 24 Yuan are paid to the two labourers for an entire season. These agricultural labourers in Sha-ku, therefore, have to take on fresh work after the middle of the ninth month, in rice planting or rice cutting, in order to make a bare living.

On the rice fields of the Sha-ku, unlike those for cane cultivation, the tenants cannot afford to hire such labourers. For, the income from rice cultivation is considerably more meagre. A tenant family of three working men and women, plus the labour force of an ox—which is either rented from or bought with money borrowed from the second or the third landlord—can usually cultivate from 70 to 80 mow, sometimes as much as 90 mow of rice. From the harvest of the first crop, 5 catties per mow are reserved for seed; and 20 catties per mow are reserved for purchasing peanut-cakes as fertilizer (for each catty of rice 5 cents' worth). With these reserves set aside, 75 per cent of the total harvest of the first and the second rice crop must be paid as the annual rent. In the district of Tung-kwan, where land fertility is very quickly decreasing, the rent, paid in grain, takes 70 per cent of the total harvest. But in the districts of Chung-shan, Pan-yu, and Shun-teh, careful inquiry shows, 75 per cent is the norm. On the dry farms of the Sha-ku, taro or potato is usually planted, and thereby the soil is turned into an easier absorbent of fertilizers. On these farms sugar cane of the variety for direct consumption is raised in the second year for the purpose of obtaining a larger income; but the tenants here must pay a higher rent, amounting to 78 per cent of the annual rice harvest. The reason why rent is paid in grain even for cane fields, seems to be twofold. A tenant family cultivating from 60 to 90 mow in the Sha-ku, where cultivation is extensive rather than intensive, hardly possesses enough cash to pay a money rent. Meantime, the second or the third landlord demands deliberately, wherever he can, payment in grain to indulge in commercial speculation.

The second or the third landlord, however, must pay a rent deposit of 2 Yuan per mow and also must pay an annual cash rent. From the original landlord to the second, to the third, or even to the occasional fourth landlord, each step usually takes an additional rent of 2 Yuan per mow. In fact, the rent in Sha-ku is paid in advance. While the harvests take place in May and in October, the cash rent is often paid in January and in July; still oftener it is paid only once a year, far in advance: at the end of every year the rent for the next year is due. Hence it is evident that the rich and the powerful alone are capable of leasing the land directly. They alone can pay the money rent in advance. In a few places of the Sha-ku, because of the recent fall of grain prices, the rent payments of January and of July have been postponed respectively to April and September; yet it still is a rent paid in advance. The two payments of the annual rent are usually divided in equal portions, but sometimes it is 40 per cent for the first time and 60 per cent for the second.

The lease from the original landlord usually extends over a tenure period of ten years. When the second or the third landlord rents out the land again, the tenure is shortened to five years or less. There are about 1,500,000 mow in the Sha-ku of Chung-shan, at least 95 per cent of which are under sub-lease in various stages. Fully one-half of this vast area is in the hands of rich merchants and powerful gentry, who, possessing superior financial resources, often are able to lease land from the clans for twenty or thirty years, sub-leasing it for periods not exceeding five years and often for only one year. However, their function is not always as purely economic as this. Allying themselves with office holders, they often manage to monopolize the land leases given out by the clans, through the use of intimidation and of force. For example, such men, with the proper backing, may threaten a higher tax assessment or even confiscation by the public authorities. Cases are known even where, during the progress of negotiations, such a group has hired mercenaries to harvest and steal a crop, in order to demonstrate their ability to make trouble, as a preliminary to negotiations with the clan for a lease at a "reasonable" rent. In short, too often what started as a bid from the vantage point of a somewhat favoured position becomes, in American parlance, a "racket"—and not even a "polite" one, at that.

Almost every renewal of the sub-leases is accompanied by an advance of the rent, till today in many places the amount collected from the final tenant is double what the original landlord receives. The position of the second and third landlord is, in fact, usually stronger than that of the original landlord who, representing a corporate body, is neither quite as free to act nor quite as keenly motivated with the desire for squeezing the last ounce of revenue from his assets. The relative standing of these lessors may be compared with that, on the one hand, of a conservative land-holding corporation in a Western country and, on the other, that of a smart "realtor." Thus it comes that the second and third landlord are often able to secure a rent rebate as high as 20 per cent on the plea of a bad harvest year and consequent inability to collect, while the final tenant, the cultivator himself, has to pay his rent in full.

With the land for producing fruit, the tenure of lease even from the second or the third landlord is usually for from 15 to 30 years. Such tenures are to be found in the third and the fifth sub-districts of Pan-yu, and the sixth and the eighth sub-districts of Chao-an. In contradistinction, the lease of rice land from the second or the third landlord, as mentioned above, is usually for three or five years, many a time for only one year, and rarely for ten years or more. When the written contract does not specify the duration of the lease, as is frequently the case in the villages of southwestern Kwangtung, this is only for the benefit of the landlord who desires to be free to change the lease, or to take back the land, at his own convenience. Where the term of the tenure of lease is undefined and there is no unwritten or implied understanding that the tenancy is intended to be permanent, the tenant is naturally reluctant to effect any improvement on the land. There is a general custom in Kwangtung, especially in the upper regions of the North River and the Han River, as well as in the southwestern part of the province, that when the rent is not in default, the lease goes on indefinitely. This custom is observed especially on clan lands. Yet even this is not in a real sense a permanent tenancy; the landlord may at any time return the rent deposit and suddenly end the lease in spite of a full payment of the rent.

It might seem that no landlord can afford to be arbitrary in shortening or lengthening a lease to suit his own purposes; for the tenants would soon find it less safe to lease his land than that of other owners, and accordingly he would find that the bids for renting his land are lower than those received by other landlords. But actually this seemingly obvious cycle of economic cause and effect, like so many others, does not take place in China. The land hunger is so great that a landlord can easily find a new tenant at any time that a lease falls in. The burden of insecurity from such arbitrariness as that here described, like every other burden of the present agrarian system, falls entirely upon the peasant class.

In a local chronicle of Kwang-ning, published in 1824, we read that many tenants have been hereditary (Vol. 12, p. 4). But at present, no permanent tenancy is found in this district. In Kao-yao, on the other hand, there seem to be some remnants of a permanent hereditary tenancy. Without previously consulting the landlord, the tenant may sub-rent the land to another tenant for cultivation; and often this sub-tenant may lease it again to a third person. Also, when a tenant from outside the clan does not pay his rent, and the landlord therefore wishes to take back the land, a certain sum of money must be paid to the retiring tenant. In some places of Meu-ming similar conditions have been observed which point to the existence of a permanent tenancy in the distant past. This remnant of a system of fair compensation for improvements may serve as a reminder that the tenant's insecurity in South China has not always been as desperate as it is today.

In Wung-yen and Ying-teh, both located in the North River Valley, there is a considerable amount of land under so-called "fertilizer-compensating" leases. Such land occupies as much as 30 per cent of the cultivated area in the northeastern corner of Ying-teh and in the southwestern corner of Wung-yuen. When such land is leased to a new tenant, he must pay his predecessor a certain amount of money; sometimes the landlord helps the old tenant to secure it. If this "compensation" is of a specified sum, the new tenant learns of it before signing the lease from his land-lord; otherwise, he has to negotiate with his predecessor. In case the old tenant demands too much, so that the transfer of the tenancy becomes a matter of dispute, the landlord steps in and compels him to come to reasonable terms. There are two theories in regard to the way in which this system of compensation has originated. It may be that in earlier days the tenant spent much labour and money on fertilizer and irrigation to improve, let us say, a piece of very poor land; and at the time of the tenancy transfer, he naturally demanded a certain sum in compensation. In the case of unusually fertile land, on the other hand, a heavy harvest is always to be expected; hence the old tenant, if the transfer takes place between harvests, naturally feels entitled to an extra payment. Of course, when this custom first arose, landlords may have objected to this, since it was apt to hinder the ready transfer of the lease. But in fear of retaliation, either in the matter of cultivation or in that of irrigation, by the old tenant, and furthermore often with real eagerness to secure the lease, the new tenant, always considers it wise to satisfy his predecessor. Regardless, then, of the origin of this system of compensation, the very fact that the so-called "fertilizer compensation" is being paid indicates a definite trace of a former right to permanent tenancy, as in the cases in Kao-yao and Meu-ming, mentioned above.

It is a remarkable fact that nothing is ever heard of permanent tenancy in the southwestern part of Kwangtung, just the sort of region where one would expect some such reminder of the old economy, because here, so far, the influence of modern commerce has been comparatively little felt. On the other hand, the custom does obtain where one would least expect it, namely in the extreme eastern part of the province, up and down the Han River where not only junks and barges but also modern steamers and a local railway ply a lively trade, carrying the modernising influence of the Swatow business world far into the interior. Indeed, in this region there are not merely remnants of a system of permanent tenancy, but a considerable part of the cultivated area is actually under this form of lease.

In the valley of the Han River there is a kind of *domaine congéable* or joint ownership of land. The landlord here often possesses only the so-called *liang-tien,* meaning the land for which tax or *liang* must be paid; and this tax responsibility is supposed to justify the rent collection. The tenant often owns what is called *chi-tien,* meaning the soil itself, or the surface. These two separate rights, one of land owning and the other of surface owning, may be mortgaged or sold independently. About two to three hundred years ago this distinction between *liang* and *chi* was very common in this region. (It is found also in other parts of China. For example, in Kiangsi it is spoken of as "bone right"—*ku-tien* and "skin right"—*pi-tien*). Just how that distinction arose, or just what is the origin of *chi-tien* would seem to require more than one single explanation. One of the accounts is that the right of *chi-tien,* that is, the right to cultivation, or the claim to permanent use of the surface of the land, derived from a long period of permanent tenancy. In past centuries high officials and big landlords used to receive cultivable but uncultivated governmental lands and leased them out to tenants. Much cost of development and primary cultivation had to be borne by those tenants; a lease contract therefore became customary under which the landlord could not transfer the tenancy. This right of permanent use of the land subsequently became a recognized object of mortgage and sale. Another widespread belief is that the *chi-tien* has originally been land owned by the peasant himself. There was a time when the land tax proper and additional taxes based upon the land became so unbearable that the peasants had to seek protection by the politically powerful families who alone could avoid taxation by controlling the tax system. By offering a certain amount of money or of grain to these families, the peasants secretly secured a tax reduction. As years went by, these "gifts" of the peasant have come to be regarded as a regular rent, and the sub-stratum has come into possession of the powerful family which now has assumed not only the function of in-betweens but of the tax payment itself. In this way the land-owning peasant became transformed into a tenant of *chi-tien,* and the taxpayer assumed the status of a landlord of *liang-tien.* Usually the price of *liang-tien* is lower than that of *chi-tien,* such as in Chao-an. Each time the land tax is advanced, the burden resting on *liang-tien* is increased; and consequently the price of *liang-tien* is constantly falling. At the point at which *liang-tien* loses so much of its value as no longer to be readily marketable it inevitably becomes combined with *chi-tien.* For the last twenty-five years, this tendency has been so strong in Chao-an that the majority of land deeds at present carry a clause to the effect that "hereby the land of unified *chi* and *liang* is completely sold", and "henceforth the land purchaser may select his own tenant." Nevertheless, 5 per cent of all the cultivated lands in the district of Chao-an are still called *chi-tien,* or lands under permanent tenancy. Many of the primary clan lands in Chao-an are still kept as *chi-tien.* The percentage of the land of permanent tenancy is higher in Mei-hsien than in Chao-an.

There is yet one other form of permanent tenure. Fully one-half of the cultivated land in the district of Mei-hsien is called *tso-tien* —a term of uncertain origin meaning—mostly in the hills, and such rented agricultural land has remained under permanent tenancy ever since the middle of seventeenth century.

CHAPTER IV

THE RENT AND PRICE OF LAND

WITH THE exception of non-irrigated lands for which in most cases a cash rent is demanded, we may say that rent payment in grain is still prevalent in Kwangtung. Shun-teh is the only district of the province where cash rent dominates; a major part of Chung-shan also pays cash rent; in Sin-hwei, Nan-hai, and Tai-shan cash rent has a spread equal to that of rent payment in grain; and in the other districts, such as Chao-an, Pan-yu, and Kai-ping, cash rent occupies only a minor part. A combination of cash and grain rent for the same land under the same lease is practically unknown in the province. While there has been a tendency, in the last ten years, to change the rent payment from grain to cash, the old method of paying rent in grain still predominates. That tendency is explainable, of course, with the increasing commercialization of crops. But quite apart from this, there is also the greater need of landlords for ready cash and, with the acute hunger for land, their growing ability to place the whole burden of risk upon the tenant while assuring themselves of a fixed income. In the present transition stage, an intermediate form of payment has made its appearance and is spreading: the landlord is paid in cash, but the amount of rent is fixed in terms of grain; that is, the actual money payment is equivalent to the value of a fixed amount of grain, estimated at the price prevailing at the time of highest quotation, in the spring.

Nevertheless, the persistence of the older form of lease is remarkable. Even in Pan-yu, where industry and commerce are more advanced than in most of the other districts, the leases stipulate neither cash rents nor the modified type of cash payment just described: they nearly always demand grain. And the reason is that the immediate landlord who collects from the peasant is not so much a dealer in land and land leases as he is a speculator in grain. Out of the 70 villages investigated in this district, only 24 have leases under which the rents are paid all in cash; 12 have the rent payments all or nearly all in grain; and the remaining 35 have the rents usually in grain. Yet none of these 70 villages is located in the Sha-ku, a region which claims one-fifth of all the cultivated lands in Pan-yu. And in this region, though the second or the third landlord pays a cash rent, the final tenant or cultivator always pays his rent in grain.

More than rice are fruit, vegetables, and cotton being commercialized. This explains why in places of rice cultivation cash rent is not so common as in places of cotton, fruit, and vegetables. In four villages of Pan-yu where only rice is planted, the area for rent in grain surpasses that for cash rent. In another group of four villages where cotton, fruit, peanuts and vegetables are grown, 96.4 per cent of the area yields a cash rent. (See table 22). In the district of Kwang-ning, three villages have been investigated; and the result shows that, while the tenants who grow bamboo pay rent in money, the rice tenants always pay it in grain. In the district of Chao-an, the rice fields yield rent in grain, and the orchards of mandarin oranges usually yield rent in money. It is to be noted in this connection that the big landlords in Si-ling, seventh sub-district of Chao-an, collect rent in grain from their orchard tenants, four piculs for each mow; rarely and only after much kowtowing may permission be secured to substitute a money rent calculated to represent a certain price of grain.

The purpose of collecting rent in grain on the part of big landlords is evidently for commercial speculation; these landlords are not satisfied with a fixed income. On the other hand, the middle peasants with sufficient means and the rich peasants who handle a commercialized crop prefer to pay their rents with a definite amount of cash; the poor peasants alone, unable to raise enough money, have to pay whatever they harvest. The statistics of ten representative villages in the district of Pan-yu indicate this clearly. Only 17 per cent of the land leased by the rich peasants brings forth rent in grain. A majority of lands cultivated by those tenants who are poor peasants, also yield such a rent. (See table 23). Almost all tenants in the Sha-ku are poor peasants; they cannot pay their rent other than in grain because, with the small amounts they have to dispose of, they cannot realize the market price.

The rent in grain may or may not be of a fixed amount. When it is not of a fixed amount, then the landlord and the tenant divide the harvest according to some definite proportion. Taking the whole province of Kwangtung, fixed rent is perhaps more prevalent than share rent. Still, the share rent prevails very widely. In Mei-hsien, share rent is paid for one-fifth of the land yielding rent in grain. This rent, locally known as *fung-li-ko*, or sharing the profit in grain, consists of several ways of dividing the harvest. In most cases the landlord takes 40 per cent, often 50 per cent, and sometimes as much as 60 per cent.

Perhaps the proportions of a share rent have some connection with the fertility of land, as well as with the means of production. This may be illustrated by the share rent in Wung-yuen, where the landlord collects a rent in grain which is 40 per cent from the best land, 50 per cent from land of medium grade, and 20 per cent from the poorest land. The share rent does not, however, depend on the fertility of the soil alone but largely on the respective amount of labour power and fertilizer which the tenant puts into the land. In this particular district, the tenant of good land often supplies more means of production per mow than other tenants because such investment is certain to pay. Improving the soil, he is actually in a better position to bargain with the landlord who cannot afford to lease his good land to tenants who cannot or will not keep up the fertility of the soil. It is for this reason that the landlord gets less rent from the tenant of the best land, paradoxical as this may seem, than he gets from the tenant of medium-grade land. One factor in the situation is the absence of highways before about 1932; this meant that some very good land was relatively inaccessible, so that in this district the landlords have had to be especially careful in the choice of tenants and thus were obliged to compromise on immediate opportunities of gain. On the other hand, when land is so poor that the value of the crop is substantially less than that from medium-grade land, the landlord obviously must content himself with a smaller return than that obtained from good land.

It will be seen, therefore, that the landlords of this region take the largest proportion of the harvest under two sets of circumstances: when rich peasants invest jointly with them in the improvement of the land, and when poor peasants have to rely on them for almost all the means of production, so that the owners can make a charge far in excess of what might be regarded as a rent for land of that quality. This latter situation happens to be illustrated by the orchards devoted to mandarin oranges in Chaoan. Here the landlord is often responsible for providing seedings and fertilizer, and then enjoys 60 per cent of the total harvest.

There is one outstanding example of share rent, for which the landlord does not at all enter into the process of production, and by which the tenant is subjected to a sort of extreme exploitation. This is to be found among the hereditary tenants generally known as *sia-wu* or servile families, often erroneously known in Western literature as "slave clans." They are not slaves in the real meaning of that word since they have the right to private property and cannot be sold. Slavery never flourished in Chinese agriculture because intensive forms of agricultural production made the use of that form of labour unprofitable. The origins of this class are not definitely known. One widespread assumption is that it represents, as similar groups do in other countries, a remnant of original inhabitants reduced by conquest to a dependence resembling serfdom. This may be true of some parts of China where such groups are found, but perhaps not of all. Another theory is that they represent the descendants of former tenant farmers who became so poor that they lost status and were eventually adopted as a hereditary labour or servant class by the clan as a whole. A third theory is that they are the descendants of bought slaves and of destitute and homeless wayfarers who voluntarily entered such service. This happens to be also the most influentially held explanation of the origins of the *Eta* class in Japan which under this "*etori* theory" is supposed to have come into being as an amalgam of members of certain despised trades (butchers, leather workers, etc.), of homeless people, and those forced, not always for ignoble reasons, to hide their identity—that is, those who because of their

57

poverty had to do the filthiest work, and the *sans famille*. To these other outcast groups were added from time to time (see Shigeaki Ninomiya, "An Inquiry Concerning the Origin, Development, and Present Situation of the *Eta* in Relation to the History of Social Classes in Japan"; in *Transaction of the Asiatic Society of Japan*, 1933, pp. 55, 72-79). In the absence of agreement among the historians, concerning the servile clans of South China, and of inability to judge which of the theories advanced is most likely to apply to the particular region here under survey, the author may be forgiven if he does not venture an explanation of his own.

Suffice it to say that in the districts of Tan-shan, En-ping, Kai-ping, and Kao-yao, there are such hereditary tenants who look upon the members of the clans that harbour them as their masters and who, in addition to farming the fields assigned to them, render additional services as labourers, servants, and watchmen, for which they are paid no wage, though here and there their wretched condition is occasionally alleviated by perquisites of various kinds.

In the village of Kwei-ling, two and one-half miles from the trading centre called Kwang-li, in the sixth sub-district of Kao-yao, there is a total population of some ten thousand, about 30 per cent of which belong to the *Sia-wu*. Here not only the landlord but also the village watchman, the "tax farmer", and some other occasional persons all have a share in the rent paid by *Sia-wu*. With this extreme class distinction at the bottom of village society there seems also to go an extreme differentiation of classes higher up. These landlords and their satellites are too proud to take a hand in agriculture at all. They feel ashamed of managing even a small orchard and live entirely on their inherited land property and such other sources of unearned increment as they may have. In contrast with landlords in other sections, they provide their tenants with nothing whatsoever for agricultural purposes; and yet the proportion of the share rent they take is very high. After every harvest their hereditary tenants—who here might almost be called their individual dependents—must gather all the grain on an open platform, before the eyes of the watchman as well as those of the landlord and the "tax farmer" who may be a merchant, or their respective representatives. The grain is divided into eleven equal piles. Of these, the landlord takes five and two-sixths, the tenant four and four-sixths, the tax collector four-sixths, and the watchman two-sixths of one pile. In percentages, 48.5 goes to the landlord, 42.4 to the tenant, 6.1 to the tax collector, and 3 to the watchman. The necessity of building dykes, which has arisen frequently in recent years to prevent floods, previously held in check by more continuous public works only adds more to the tenant's burden; for an extra portion of his harvest is now taken for dyke building. At present, of the eleven piles the landlord gets four and four-sixths, the tenant retains only four, the tax collector still gets four-sixths, and the watchman still gets two-sixths of one pile. The remaining one and two-sixths of a pile are set aside to pay for the dykes. Again in percentages, the landlord has 42.4, the tenant has now only 36.4, the dyke fee claims 12.1, and the tax collector and the watchman still retain 6.1 and 3 respectively.

By such a system of share rent, an attempt seems to be made to disguise further exploitation of the tenant. Apparently the landlord takes less, but actually the tenant pays more, because the burden of tax responsibility is shifted from the landlord's shoulders upon his. While the landlord's share has seemingly been reduced from 48.5 to 42.4 per cent, the proportion of the crop which the tenant actually has to give up has increased from 57.6 to 63.6 per cent. Land tax and dyke fee, according to the usual way of taxation, should be paid out of the rent itself; but now the burden of both is shifted from the landlord to the tenant.

By the system of share rent, tax has become an additional rent, and the landlord easily shakes off his tax obligations. The world in general has always understood that a share rent rests more lightly upon the tenant than a fixed rent; but this instance shows that this form of rent also can be so manipulated as to crush the tenant farmer. There are, moreover, other concealed matters in this system which prove detrimental to the tenant. For instance, the landlord and the tax collector often bring with them armed bodyguards to pile up the grain. They take not only, as we have seen, more piles but bigger piles, which are sometimes—believe it or not—twice as big as those left to the cultivator himself.

Under the system of a fixed rent in grain, the tenant often fares no better. In Hwei-yang and in the neighbouring district Hai-fung, for instance, there is the *Tso-ke* system which necessitates an extra rent payment. A *Tso-ke* is simply a descendant of a rich merchant or powerful official who was able to protect the small landowner against heavy taxation by having the power to defy government authorities. As a price for the protection, the small landowner used to offer him a certain amount of grain every year, which in the course of time has come to be considered as a regular rent. That is, after a time, the *Tso-ke* took up the whole responsibility for payment of the land tax, and what had been a fee for protection now became a rent for the use of the land. The landowner may sell his land, and the *Tso-ke* may independently sell his right to this particular rent. The *tso-ke* pays a land tax amounting to only 2½ per cent of the rent he collects; all the rest of the rent he is able to keep. It happens that the size of mow in Hwei-yang and Hai-fung is larger than in other districts; it is by 30 per cent larger than the standard mow. Two harvests every year in Hwei-yang yield 3 piculs of unhusked rice per standard mow. Out of this, the tenant has to pay to the landowner one and six-tenths of a picul and to the *Tso-ke* two-tenths of a picul. While only 5 per cent of a picul per standard mow is paid as land tax, the fixed rent in grain paid by the tenant amounts to 60 per cent of the total harvest.

In Tai-shan, 70 per cent of the tenants pay a fixed rent in grain, which is about 50 per cent of the crop. In the districts of North River Valley, such as Loh-chang and Kuh-kiang, the amount is considerably less. In the southwestern part of the province it is often much more. Hoh-pu is a good example; the fixed rent in grain predominates here. In a few cases the grain is paid once a year after the harvest of the second crop; but it is paid usually twice a year: 40 per cent after the first crop and 60 per cent after the second. This fixed rent is at least 30 per cent of the crop, but in a great majority of cases it is as much as 60 per cent. In the vicinity of Chang-huang, in the northern part of Hoh-pu, where the hilly lands are not rocky but very fertile, a higher productivity has created a higher rent. For, after paying 60 per cent of grain as a fixed rent, the tenant here still makes regular presents to his landlord. The fixed rent in grain in Lien-kiang, a district immediately east of Hoh-pu, is usually 65 per cent of the total harvest. It is not unusual, therefore, to hear of tenants in Lien-kiang who sell their children in order to pay the rent. Boys or girls of ten years of age are being sold for less than 100 Yuan per capita. (The value of currency in Kwangtung is lower than in

North China; a local Yuan is about 70 and sometimes 80 per cent of the standard Yuan, such as is found in Shanghai. All our figures relating to rents, taxes, prices, interests, and wages in Kwangtung are understood to be in the local Yuan).

Immediately east of Lien-kiang are the districts of Wu-chwan and Hwa-hsien, where the landlords have the reputation of adopting the severest measures for rent collection. In Wu-chwan, when rent is in default for the first year, a monthly interest is charged on it of from 3 to 5 per cent. Should the rent be in default for another year, the landlord would employ ruffians to extract as much as they can toward the payment for rent as well as for interest. These tools or claws of the landlords are locally known as *Lan-tze,* meaning "corrupt and unprincipled people." They often snatch away labour animals from the luckless tenant, and sometimes even take from him a boy or a girl to cover the debt. In Hwa-hsien, the landlord usually bribes some soldiers to collect the rent for him. For getting a rent of three-tenths of a picul, which amounts to 0.60 Yuan, the men in uniform are rewarded with 6.00 Yuan; in other words, the tenant must pay eleven times the original rent. One of the Hwa-hsien tenants sold in 1929 his son of nine years of age for 120 Yuan; two years later he had to sell another son of five years for 90 Yuan; and again two years later he sold his daughter of six years for 70 Yuan; every time the money was used to pay rent and debt. So every year, early in the spring, the extortion of back rents calls forth a sale of children.

A part of Pan-yu also has fixed rent in grain; its amount is ordinarily 55 per cent of the harvest and rarely exceeds 60 per cent. In the districts of Lien-hsien, Ju-yuen, Jen-hwa, and Wung-yuen, all located in North River Valley, the amount of fixed rent in grain is somewhat smaller, usually 40 per cent of the harvest. Only in a few places of Ying-teh and Nan-hsiung does it amount to 50 per cent. With the exceptions of Fung-shun, where it is 30 per cent of the produce, of Chiao-ling, where it is 35 per cent, and of Hsing-ning and Wu-hwa, where it is 40 per cent, the eastern portion of Kwangtung, generally speaking, has a fixed rent in grain, amounting to one-half of the harvest. In the valley of West River, generally speaking, such a rent is from 40 to 60 per. cent. The proportion of rent paid in grain is largest in relation to the harvest, as we have seen above in the districts of southwestern Kwangtung.

Suppose we figure out the value of the fixed rent in grain according to its market price, we should be able to tell how many years of rent payment would equal the price of land from which the rent is collected. For example, if one mow of land in Kai-ping is 280 Yuan, and from it is derived a rent in grain valued at 16 Yuan, then seventeen and a half years of this rent cover the land price. These seventeen and a half years may be called "purchase periods." The number of years in such periods indicates the relative speed of property accumulation on the part of the landlord. The longer purchase periods signify slower accumulation, and the shorter ones quicker accumulation. In Kai-ping, the purchase periods are from seventeen and a half to twenty years, in Sin-hsing they are from eleven to sixteen and a half, in Kao-yao from eleven to fourteen, and in Kai-tien from eleven to thirteen and a half years.

These differences reflect not so much variations in the condition of the land as the relative ability of the owners in different regions to derive gain from the prevailing land hunger, and also the competition for land as an investment. Thus, for example, in regions where large remittances are received from family members overseas, the price of land will be comparatively high in relation to rent, and the "purchasing periods" will be long. On the other hand, in the extreme south-western part of the province, more remote from contacts with the world of trade and finance, but where nevertheless a dense population demands land, we find comparatively high rents in relation to the price of land, and the purchasing periods are short—in spite of the fact that much of the land is of poor quality. In this south-western corner of Kwangtung, the purchasing periods are from fifteen to sixteen years in Ling-shan, from ten to fourteen in Hoh-pu, from eleven to thirteen in Kin-hsien, and from ten to twelve in Fan-cheng. While the tenants sometimes have to part with their children to pay the rent, the landlords, without any participation in production, may even double their land possessions in ten years.

Where the rent in grain is prevailing, cash rent is not so high as rent in grain. For, in such a place, cash rent is collected only from non-irrigated lands, of lower productivity; the amount of this cash rent is sometimes 15 per cent less than the rent in grain. On the other hand, where the rent in cash is more common, as in the districts of Pan-yu, Sin-hwei, Nan-hai, Shun-teh, and Chung-shan, the rent in grain is lower than the cash rent, sometimes by 10 per cent. In these districts, cash rents help the landlords to accumulate property very rapidly. The purchase periods in Nan-hai and in San-shui are from nine to eleven years shorter than those in any of the southwestern districts. In the regions of Chung-shan, which are outside of the Sha-ku, the price of *Kang-tien,* or the lands in fertile valleys, is usually 300 Yuan per mow, for which a cash rent of 30 Yuan must be paid.

Sometimes cash rent in Kwangtung amounts to more than one-half of the total cost of production. This may be seen from a budget account of sugar cane fields in Pan-yu, as reported by the Agricultural College of the National University of Kwangtung in 1925. The cost of production per mow of sugar cane in the Sha-ku of Pan-yu is as follows:

For the first year	Yuan	For the second year	Yuan
Rent	17.00	Rent	17.00
Hired Labour	6.00	Hired Labour	5.00
Seedlings, 1,400 pieces	5.60	Peanut-cake fertilizer,	
Peanut-cake fertilizer,		120 catties	6.60
150 catties	8.25		

Thus, the total cost of production per mow, for 1,600 catties of millable sugar, is 65.45 Yuan; and the rent amounts to more than one-half of this total.

From the rice fields of the Sha-ku, the rent collection amounts to as much as 71 per cent of the total harvest. While the income per mow is about 18 Yuan, what the tenant must pay as rent includes 12 Yuan of the rent proper, 0.50 Yuan for the supposed watchman, 0.12 Yuan for the hypothetical introducer of the lease, and another 0.12 Yuan for the theoretical subsidy to the rent collector under the charming name of "expenditure for shoes." Besides, there is an additional rent claimed by the primary land-lord; and this is based on the property right over sea waters adjacent to the field, which are regarded as potential lands. Locally this right is known as *Sha-kuo-chuan* ("property of the sand bank"), or *Ya-pu* ("place for raising ducks"), or *Yu-shua-pu* ("place for catching fishes and shrimps"). When the primary landlord in the Sha-ku sells his land near the sea instead of charging a higher rent for the special economic advantage, he reserves this as a separate property right, upon which he charges a special annual sur-rent of from 0.05 to 0.10 Yuan per mow. Such a traditional idea of property in shore rights is still upheld by the courts today. In 1932, Ta-shih and Hwei-kiang, two villages in the Sha-ku of Pan-yu, disputed over the former's right of building dykes in a place where the latter's *Sha-kuo-chuan* was still claimed. Though the provincial court of Kwangtung did not think that the *Sha-kuo-chuan* should prevent the building of dykes, it nevertheless upheld this property right and ordered the clan of Ta-shih to pay an annual rent to the clan of Hwei-kiang. In this case, 200 Yuan are to be paid every year for the shore rights of an area of 300 mow.

The excessive amount of rent has undoubtedly hindered the agricultural development of this fertile region of the Sha-ku. Some of the rich peasants here used to lease very much land, and many agricultural labourers whom they used to hire have always lived together in a big house, known as *Kwei-kwan,* or an "enclosed establishment." Often the entire farm, which thirty years ago may have been over 1,000 mow, has been called by this same name. The usual production of grain per mow, thirty years ago, was 6 piculs of unhusked rice; now it has decreased to only 4 piculs, because with the higher rent it is no longer possible to put the same amount of labour or improvement into the soil. The rent paid at that time was 6 Yuan per mow; now it is 12 Yuan. During three decades, while the productivity has been cut by one-third, the amount of rent has been doubled. The falling of prices of agricultural products, the relatively slow drop of wages and especially the rapid advance of rents, all have worked together to diminish the size of *Kwei-kwan*. In Chang-chow and its vicinity, the *Kwei-kwan* has shrunk on an average from 1,000 to 500 or 400 mow; and in order to maintain such an enterprise, a part of this reduced area must be devoted to orchards which yield a better income. In a few places where the large farm, or the *Kwei-kwan,* can not plant orchards, there must be a second ploughing for a more abundant second crop of rice, instead of the usual practice of *Tsan-kao*. Some years ago, there used to be a few *Kwei-kwan* south of Chang-chow, but they have gone out of existence entirely.

How does it come that rents go up and up, while all the other claims on the product of agriculture have to content themselves with less and less? How does it come that the landlord apparently is exempted from bearing his part of the loss brought about by falling prices? The chief answer to this riddle is that the product of rural enterprise is forced to support an ever larger and heavier super-structure of non-productive elements. Taxes in South China always increase and, sometimes, at a calamitous rate. The landlord, now more often an absentee than he was even a generation ago, lives in an environment of modern habits of luxury and social ambitions. If, for the moment, we personify the class, we may imagine him as a business man living in Canton, perhaps once in a long while attending some ceremony at the ancestral temple, but otherwise taking very little personal interest in the village and neighbourhood which produces his rents. The higher are the taxes he has to pay on the land he owns, and the more rapidly these rise, the more anxious he will be to guard himself against possible loss from this source by every conceivable device to squeeze more income from his land. And he alone of all those who share in the product of the agricultural enterprise is able thus to fortify his position because, with other members of his class, he controls the political power, both local and provincial. Suppose the tenant is in arrears: our landlord has all the forces of law and order behind him if he decides that it is best to evict the tenant and to take back the land with all the improvements the tenant may have made. Or, on the other hand, he also has the authorities on his side if he decides to tide over the tenant by forcing him into a loan agreement or into the signing of a new lease which puts him completely into the hands of his creditor, the landlord himself. Suppose, assuming the landlord to be also a direct employer, that his labourers can no longer make a living and become bandits. He has at his disposal the police and military power of the district and, if need be, of the whole province; or he can hire a gang of his own to beat the workers into submission without anyone being able to stay his hands. And the source of all this power is, of course, the fact that so far, in an as yet predominantly rural society, the landlord class alone possesses an essential monopoly for the use of which it can make its own terms.

Some believe that the helplessness of the Chinese peasants is caused by the smallness of their holdings and the consequent weakness of the producers in their dealings with the owners of the land. The idea as repeatedly been advanced that farming might again prosper in China with the introduction of farming enterprise on a large scale and commercially organized. That idea, in the light of our findings in Kwangtung, must appear unrealistic, so long as even at a time of disastrously declining prices for agricultural products there is no sign of a fall in rents. To take a concrete example, the havoc wrought by high rents may clearly be discerned in the present situation in Shun-teh. In this famous silk district, 70 per cent of the cultivated land is covered with mulberries. For both the mulberry and the rice lands, in Shun-teh, cash rent is being paid, which in the course of the last thirty years has become a rent paid nearly always in advance. The amount of this rent is anywhere from 6 to 50 Yuan per mow, usually from 20 to 25 Yuan. Within the last three years, the average price of cocoons per catty has dropped from 2.00 to 0.30 Yuan; consequently, the price of mulberries per picul has dropped from 5.00 to 0.60 Yuan, when 0.60 or 0.65 Yuan per picul has to be paid as a wage for leaf picking. Under such conditions, many mulberry peasants prefer not to pick the leaves. Now, seven crops of mulberries are expected in Shun-ter every year; when the leaves of one crop are left unpicked, those of the next naturally become tough and therefore cannot be sold. Hence, at least 30 per cent of the mulberry fields have been abandoned. The peasants own less than 10 per cent of all the mulberry fields; and many a tenant has to pay a rent even for the abandoned land. Moreover, according to the custom of Shun-teh, the tenant must pay the land tax for his landlord, which is later deducted from his rent payment. The Shun-teh tenants are now being pursued not only by the landlord, but also by the tax collector. The prices of silk and cocoons are so unremunerative that peasants throw the silkworms into ponds to feed the fish: men suffer hunger while fish are well nourished. The fish may be sold; but even so, the tenants can hardly afford to eat rice-gruel twice a day; how can they pay the rent? The landlord would never cancel it, the best he would do is to grant a rent reduction. Such a reduction may be as high as 50 per cent; but for the tenant it can only mean a further indebtedness.

Of late, some of the mulberry land has been turned into sugar-cane fields; but the price of sugar—which is inevitably determined by that of Java and Formosa—offers no more secure basis for the livelihood of these Chinese peasants than did their previous principal cash crop. So, yet another suggestion has been made, namely, that of transforming the mulberry fields into rice fields. The necessary expenditure for this purpose, however, is definitely prohibitive; for, even without considering the required new implements, the cost of such a change would be at least 25 Yuan per mow, in some cases as much as 50 Yuan. A more reasonable plan would be to transform mulberry fields into grain fields other than rice. In that case, the cost involved would be much smaller, yet the comparatively meagre income from such crop can hardly meet one-half of the present rent.

Rent reduction in Kwangtung has taken place only in Shun-teh and in one or two neighbouring silk districts. Taking the province as a whole, the amount of rent has evidently increased within five years. Of course, where harvests turn out to be extraordinarily bad, there have been some discounts for the rent; but on the average, it has been increased in five years by 20 per cent. In the *Annual* of the Tan-shan District Government for 1933, we find that the rent per mow of first-grade land in that district was 20 Yuan in 1928, but has been increased to 30 Yuan by 1933. Such a rent increase of 50 per cent in half a decade may be taken as the factor which more than any other has prevented the Tai-shan peasants from adopting the cultivation of an extra winter crop. (See the *Annual,* p. 33 of General Section and p. 6 of Special Section).

The explanation for this situation probably is a complicated one. The main cause is that land prices in this region have gone up enormously in recent years because, with the world economic depression and the corresponding improvement in the Chinese exchange rate, remittances from Chinese overseas have suddenly and greatly increased. To be more specific, thousands of Tai-shan's sons in the United States and elsewhere have, in addition to their usual remittances for the support of relatives at home, sent large sums for investment in their home community or neighbourhood; and since the times were unpropitious for industrial or other forms of capitalistic enterprise, a large part of these savings found its way into land purchase, producing something of a boom. At first, such a rise in prices may not affect the position of the tenants; but with each new transfer the owner, having purchased at a higher price than the previous one, will naturally endeavour to reduce the purchase period by raising the rent. Another reason for the abnormal rent increases in this region is that, also as a result of the world economic depression, many small Chinese business men or truck gardeners could no longer make a living abroad and decided to come home. The return of large numbers of these men undoubtedly raised the demand for use of land, whether by purchase or by lease, producing yet another—more direct if smaller— tendency to raise rents.

A slight and gradual increase in rents might have induced the peasants of this region to make an extra effort to increase production in the direction suggested by the local authorities in the report just quoted. But the increase in the rents was so overwhelming that it had the opposite psychological effect: instead of stimulating the tenants to greater effort, it made them fear that any addition to the product from their holding would merely invite the landlord to grab more by further rent increases.

A not dissimilar sequence of events has been observed in a big village named Ya-hu, in the northern part of Pan-yu, where 60 per cent of the cultivated lands are clan lands. Within the last three years, many of the Yahu emigrants have returned from Canada; the competition for leasing clan lands has consequently been intensified. The rent per mow has increased to 20 Yuan, whereas three years ago it used to be 12 Yuan, indicating an advance of 66 per cent in a very short period.

The increase of the tax burden, especially in the last few years, also has been shifted on to the tenant in the form of an increase in rent. In fact, the tenant is not able to distinguish between tax and rent. The total amount of taxes paid by the landlord in the sixth sub-district of Ling-shan is now three times the land tax proper. This has directly led to further increases in rent which, however, have not been uniform. The rent in grain per mow for the best land has recently increased from 0.12 to 0.15 picul, for the land of medium grade from 0.10 to 0.13 picul, and for the poorest land from 0.08 to 0.10 picul. Here the total harvest on the best land, two crops in a year, yields only 4 piculs per mow. The tenants found these rent increases so unbearable that they took the first opportunity to beseech the Government to intervene and to order the landlords to reduce rents. However, they were unable to prevail against the landlords since many of these, possessing anywhere from 2,000 to 6,000 mow, maintain a political influence which no one can help recognizing. An administrative conference of all sub-district officers of Ling-shan was held on January 15 to 18, 1934; and to this many representatives of tenants throughout the district made a joint petition for rent reduction; but since the Government has to rely upon the big landlords in every way for taxation, the opinions of these men have to be respected, and rent reduction has not been approved. This illustrates why both here and also in Chekiang Province efforts of the Kuomintang to secure rent reductions by ordinance, or through setting up committees to arbitrate between landlords and tenants, have failed. Since they were not in a position of first reducing taxes but, on the contrary, like almost all local and provincial authorities in China, are asking for more and more public revenue, these authorities and party officials could not insist on rent reductions on the part of the land-lords: so long as these are among the largest taxpayers, they have the upper hand whenever it comes to a show-down.

Much has been promised by the Provincial Government of Kwangtung to help the peasants by establishing new sugar factories. One fact, however, has been brought to light: that when rice fields are transformed into sugar cane fields, the rent invariably is just as suddenly increased. Before the first factory located in Hwei-yang was in full operation, the governmental authorities had already found it necessary to "forbid rent increases within three square miles from the factory in the next four years." Such an official proclamation does not, however, prevent such action on the part of the landlord; and before the expected higher income is in sight, the tenant has to face a raise in his rent.

The establishment of sugar factories, in this instance, is paralleled by other economic advantages which theoretically should redound to the advantage of the producers, and historically no doubt often have done so. Take, for example, the enormous advantage which the peasants in districts near the seaboard and the port cities enjoy in marketing their products, in comparison with those inland. Such farmers often receive from four to ten times as much for their crops as do those in the interior who are handicapped by the lack of inexpensive transportation facilities to the coast. (See, for example, some figures given by R. Feng in his article on "Agriculture" in the *Symposium on Chinese Culture,* published by the

China Institute of Pacific Relations—original editions Shanghai 1931, p. 229). In the old days, the peasants of Kwangtung seem actually to have retained for their own benefit a large part of this advantage—as witness the ruins of so many magnificent stonebuilt villages in the Pearl River Delta region. But an increased mobility of trade capital, unaccompanied by a corresponding mobility of labour, has meant that in recent times the benefit has flown entirely into non-productive channels.

Some of the Chinese literati have put all the blame for such conditions as these on the shoulders of the tenant. In the local chronicle of Chung-shan, published in 1879 (Vol. 5, p. 19), we find this comment:

"People are so tricky, rents are usually in default, early every winter the landlord has to demand the rent for next year. During times of civil war, when communications are cut and the price of grain is consequently increased, the tenant reaps a big profit, and his income is frittered away in luxury. But a subsequent fall of grain prices hits all the peasants, who cannot again be frugal. It makes them compete in renting in land. In the hope for a full harvest or for better prices of grain, they are willing to pay higher rents. In a few years, the tenants themselves become bankrupted; and on this account the landlords also suffer. No wonder that the spirit of propriety is fast dying out."

But the reality is so: while the tenant is not able to pay his rent, the landlord transforms the rent in grain into a cash rent to be paid in advance; while the grain price drops and with it also the income of the tenant who must then face a rent in default, the landlord increases the rent in order to maintain his total income. The peasants compete to lease parcels of land out of sheer necessity and not at all for profit; in fact, the more the ownership of the land is concentrated, the keener becomes the competition of would-be tenants. There is no market price for agricultural land as this would be understood in a Western nation; that is, there is little or no mobility, and it makes all the difference to the relative economic strength of lessor and lessee whether the cultivable land of a given neighbourhood is in many or in few hands. Lack of a standard price and therefore standard rent level, and inability, under Chinese social conditions, to move away, leave the tenant at the mercy of the local landlords unless there are enough of these in the community, in proportion to the number of would-be lessees, to produce some competition for tenants and so to enable these to play out one landlord against the other. The progressive concentration of land ownership in Kwangtung during recent years has been clearly reflected in the continuous increase of rent.

We have already seen that the increase in the price of land is not uniform or, indeed, ubiquitous in the region under review. For example, in those districts where remittances from overseas have caused a competition for land purchase, naturally the price of land has gone up to an extraordinary height. In the 5th Ku of Kao-yao, one mow of the best land costs no less than 500 Yuan; a few years ago it has been over 1,000 Yuan. Though in recent years house rent and the real estate property in Sun-ning, the district city of Tai-shan, have greatly fallen in value, the prices of agricultural lands in this district have not shown any change; for a single mow of medium grade land, one still has to pay about 300 Yuan sometimes even as much as 1,200. In the southern part of Tai-shan, near Kwang-hai, the land price has gone up by 20 per cent in the last five years. Perhaps the highest land price in Kwangtung is to be found in Mei-hsien; in Nan-kow-pao of the 3rd Ku of this district, at least 500 Yuan must be paid for one local unit of the best land. Now, the local unit is called *tan,* a little less than one third of the standard mow. The price of one mow, therefore, is about 1,600 Yuan. Mei-hsien claims a percentage of land-owning peasants higher than in almost any other district in the province, and witnesses a comparatively smaller volume of land sales; consequently it has not been very much affected by the recent decline of remittances from overseas.

Of course, because of the increased tax burden, the decreased value of rice, and the collapse of the silk and cocoon industry, the land prices in many localities have actually fallen. But on the contrary, in many other places, because of the competitive purchases of land by the *noveaux riches,* they have risen. The recent development in Hoh-pu suffices to illustrate this. The local unit of cultivated land here is called *tou,* which is about one-half of the standard mow. The price of one *tou* of land in Hoh-up was 15 Yuan in 1910, 25 in 1921, 30 in 1926, and 35 in 1929. Within the last five years the land price has risen continuously, until at present one *tou* of medium-grade land costs 40 and that of the best quality at least 50 Yuan. Land prices are especially high on the delta of Lo-cheng-kiang, in the extreme southwestern corner of Hoh-pu.

Here, in the last three years, the average price of land in the villages of Sha-kang, Chun-an, and Chien-tie, have increased by more than one-half. The usual price of one *tou* on this delta has reached 120 Yuan; in other words, it costs 240 Yuan per standard mow. In the 5th Ku of Hoh-pu, especially in the vicinity of Nan-kong, the price is also rapidly rising. Until recent years, the peasants who cultivate their own land have constituted more than one-half of the peasant families in this Ku; but now they are reduced to only about 30 per cent. Generally speaking, nearly 10 per cent of all the peasant families in Hoh-pu are hired out as year-labourers. Their usual annual wage is 30 Yuan; and if they are paid in grain, that wage is of even less value.

The magistrate of Hoh-pu, Liao-Yung-cheng, has told that, of the *nouveaux riches* who have bought the lands in Nan-kong and on the Lo-cheng-kiang delta, 20 per cent are merchants and 80 per cent are high civil and military officers. We thus see that with inevitable logic concentration of ownership also means absentee ownership. The human counterpart of the phenomenon which we have endeavoured to describe in this chapter in terms of rents and prices is the disruption of that rural society which has persisted in China for so many centuries and which certain writers, blind to the realities, wish to persuade the world to regard as one destined to live on forever as the only system congenial, to quote a favourite phrase, to the spirit of the race. Actually, all classes are perhaps equally eager to escape from the present intolerable situation by following into the towns the landlords and the larger merchants and, on the other end of the social scale, the footless labourers; but this they cannot do. Though the inherited love of the soil, under present circuumstances, tends to disappear, the necessity of coaxing some sort of living from it remains for that great majority, the middle and small peasants.

CHAPTER V

TAXES, TOLLS, AND TORTS

IN APRIL, 1933, the office of the Pacification Commission in Kwangtung, to which was delegated the task of exterminating the Communist movement, made, by its 808th order, the following proclamation:

"The work of reconstruction in this province has been steadily progressing during the last few years; the burden on the people also is getting increasingly heavy. Numerous tax bureaux have been established in every locality, extracting money under all sorts of cleverly named surtaxes, and making requisitions for various pretended military purposes. These miscellaneous levies far exceed the tax proper; they satisfy the rapacity of the local gentry, but hardly at all contribute toward the cost of public works. This condition must be alleviated, if the people's ability to pay taxes is to be preserved."

In May of the same year, the military governor of the province inspected the districts of East River and Han River. In his report to the Southwestern Political Council, he honestly stated his understanding:

"The financial resources of these districts are taxes of four categories: the sur-tax, the production tax, the transit tax, and the assessment. All of them have been initiated to meet urgent demands, without considering their desirability, their legality, or the principle of equality. This simply opens up a new avenue for the local gentry to acquire more wealth. I realize, therefore, that the present system of taxation not only lays a burden on the workers and the peasants, but also gives birth to a new group of greedy gentry."

The military governor here neglected to mention the tax collecting merchant, or tax farmer who, once the Government has accepted his bid, thereby monopolizes the collection. The actual sums collected by these agents are several times, sometimes as much as ten times, what the Government receives. This almost unbelievable statement has been verified in a number of instances. Of course, it must be realized that it does not imply a fantastically successful peculation and enrichment of a few individuals: as taxes and tolls multiply, a whole army of collectors spring into being to prey upon the people, none of them big men as rascals go in China, but, although each overcharges by 500 or even 900 per cent, more like a swarm of locusts than a herd of bisons. The numerous taxes imposed by both provincial and district governments, such as sales and transit taxes on oil, on hemp, on hide, on fish, on fruit, on cow, on ox, on pig, on sausages and on dried mushrooms, verily provide these tax merchants with their El Dorado. For the monopoly of collecting one or several of these taxes, a company is usually organized. "The Lee-yuan Company for collecting taxes on ox butchering, and on the export of ox-hides, of oxen and of pigs in the Hwei-chow region" may serve as an example.

This sort of tax collecting company has in reality become an administrative bureau. Under the pretext of maintaining order in those places where taxes are being collected and of assuring the tax income, it issues independent ordinances and even organizes a system of armed inspectors and detectives. These people wear neither badge nor uniform and, of course, easily abuse their power. The schools in Kwangtung also have assumed the air of financial bureaus. In Loh-chang, for instance, the First Primary Public School has issued the following proclamation, dated April 18th, 1934, and signed by its principal, a Mr. Hsu-chung:

"The public is hereby notified that, with official permission of the District Government, this school has in recent years been collecting a sur-tax on the houses of prostitution, both on the land and on the river; and that as its agency of collection this school has now authorized Lee Hung-chun, a merchant who has organized the Heng-yu Company for this purpose."

All these taxes eventually fall on the shoulders of the peasants even when these do not themselves consume the commodities or use the services taxed.

Ever since 1932, under the banner of rural self-government, numerous administrative bureaus for the *Ku,* the *Chung,* and the *Hsiang*—different constituent administrative regions of a district—

have been established. In order to finance them, the tax burden is further increased. The major income of the Ku and the Hsiang bureaus in Chung-shan comes from a family tax, a land sur-tax, a vegetable-weighing tax, a tax for the watchmen on *Sha-tien,* and sometimes also an export tax on fish and shrimps. (This "export" tax is, of course, a unilateral local transit tax and has nothing to do with the ultimate destination of the commodity). Some of the Ku bureaus themselves possess *sha-tien* (agricultural land in the Sha-ku) and derive their income from the rent. Even after *sha-tien* is sold out, a rent on *Sha-kuo-chuan* may be collected at the rate of one tenth of a picul per mow after each harvest. The basis of existence for all the Ku bureaus in Mei-hsien also is a series of taxes, such as both licence and sales taxes on gambling and on opium smoking, assessments on temples and monasteries, licence taxes on religious feasts, wedding ceremonies, and on pig butcherings, transfer taxes on land sales and land mortgages. Widows are permitted to marry again only after paying a fee of 6 Yuan, and this fee also goes to support the Ku bureau. In Yuh-nan, the sur-taxes added to the existing fees for pig and ox butchering and the new taxes on the "export" of chickens, ducks, fish, firs and pines, usually suffice to maintain the Ku bureaus in ger. ': but the bureau of the 6th Ku, with a monthly budget of 660 Yuan, i being financed particularly by a sur-tax in grain on every mow of cultivated land in that sub-district. Some of the Ku bureaus in Kwangtung have a monthly budget of over 1,000 Yuan; that of Kwang-hai-ku in the district of Tai-shan, which takes 0.40 Yuan per picul from the "export" of salted fish to supply 90 per cent of its funds, has an expenditure of 2,000 Yuan a month. Although export taxes, so-called, are simply transit levies on agricultural products going out of the locality, they are often collected under a fictitious name, such as the "inspection fee" in Hwei-yang. Undoubtedly the "inspection" has gone far enough when at the periodical village markets, 0.02 or 0.03 Yuan is levied for every 100 eggs.

Although the building of new public roads in Kwangtung in the past few years has improved communication and has thus facilitated military movements, it has imposed upon the peasantry a heavy burden, just as it has done in many other provinces. Perhaps a few examples may suffice to make this clear. During

1928, in the village of Mei-tien, Pan-yu, 0.10 Yuan per mow was assessed for road building; and in that same year, in the village of Tang-yai, within three miles on each side of the road, every man and woman had to contribute 2.50 Yuan. From Shih-liu to Sin-tsao a new public road passes through or by nearly one hundred villages, each of which has had to pay for it at the rate of 0.30 Yuan per mow. Further South, this road runs from Sin-tsao to Shi-chiao; and for this track every man in every village has had to pay 2.00 Yuan. A similar assessment upon the males of the village Pei-shan caused many of the men to run away; as a result, each of those who remained had to pay even more. There are plenty of other examples outside of Pan-yu. In Ying-teh, 1.40 Yuan used to be paid on every unit of cultivated land for road building. In Chao-an, 2.00 Yuan used to be paid for every mow. During 1931, in the 6th sub-district of Kao-yao, as much as 4.00 Yuan per capita was assessed for road building alone. The next year, in the 3rd sub-district of Hwa-hsien, immediately north of Pan-yu, every adult male was ordered to pay 6.00 Yuan for a public road. The villages tried hard to dodge this tax, and even organized themselves to oppose it. Troops were sent to subdue them, their leaders were imprisoned, and finally they had to pay according to the governmental orders.

These impositions must be distinguished from taxes levied in such districts as Tai-shan and Chung-shan for making roads which actually aid civilian communication and, among other things, enlarge the market for agricultural products. In these cases, which as yet are rare, the road tax may be regarded as an assessment for an improvement, largely of public benefit, though perhaps the payment is burdensome at the time. Unfortunately, even in these cases, however, confiscation of land, arbitrary transit franchises for the benefit of the few and the detriment of the many, and exorbitant tolls, only a small part of the income from which reaches its destined purpose, too often mar what started as a public-spirited enterprise. The majority of road taxes in Kwangtung are not for improvements of any kind, from the farmer's point of view.

The most secluded and mountainous district of Wung-yuen, in the North River Valley, is now reached by two public roads: one from Kiangsi and the other from the Hankow-Canton railway line in Ying-teh. The road from Wung-yuen to Ying-teh was built between 1928 and 1932 at a total cost of more than 800,000 Yuan This was met from the following resources: 150,000 of sur-tax on land, issue of 250,000 of unredeemable paper notes, 160,000 from "contributions" of the rich gentry, and, what was felt most immediately as a burdensome pressure, 250,000 Yuan of poll tax, at the rate of 1 Yuan per head, regardless of sex, on persons from one to fifty years old. The road from Wung-yuen to Kiangsi, work on which began in 1933, also was built by extra taxes: 1.20 Yuan was assessed for every unit of cultivated land throughout the district. At present, the road to Ying-teh is monopolized by a motor bus company which has taken the "contributions" of the rich gentry as its stock shares. This same company is now collecting for the district government an "export" tax on all agricultural products from fifty catties up, at the rate of 0.05 Yuan for every fifty catties. The public road built through taxation proves to be a new instrument for further taxation.

Often agricultural lands have been confiscated, or nearly confiscated, because of road building; after having been heavily taxed for this purpose, they are incorporated in the road area without payment. In Hwei-yang, a road of twenty-five miles from Tan-sui to Ping-hu was built by virtually confiscating the adjoining agricultural lands. Only one-tenth of the area occupied by this road is of hilly land, three-tenths of cultivable lands, and six-tenths of already well cultivated lands. In the beginning one-half of the market price of the land, which is little enough, had been promised to the owners; but later the payment was made in the form of stock shares of the motor bus company which was to operate on this road. The annual net income of the company has been around 60,000 Yuan; no interest, however, has ever been distributed to the stock holders. What is worse for the land owners, most of whom are small peasants, is that after the disguised confiscation of their lands they still have to pay land tax. Many such cases may be cited; a few most remarkable ones are in Kuh-kiang, Loh-chang, and Chao-an. As most of the confiscated lands belong to unorganized small peasants, their feeble attempts to protest are of no avail. In the vicinity of Canton, agricultural lands have been confiscated not only because of road building, but also by unexpected orders of military and civil authorities to establish some real or fictitious public institutions, experimental agricultural stations and charitable homes being a favourite form of such deceit. The villages of Shih-pai and Tang-yai can best testify to this. In some cases, the Government has made a promise to pay from 80 to 100 Yuan per mow, according to the grades of the land; but while this promise remains unfulfilled, the authorities keep on collecting the land tax year after year. Thus, one of the Hsiang chiefs named Chien has lost his 13 mow of very fertile land, valued at more than 3,000 Yuan, and still has to pay more than 1 Yuan per mow as the land tax.

In the process of public road building, land confiscation is accompanied by conscription of labour. The process by which the road from Pan-yu to Tseng-cheng was built during the two years of 1928 and 1929, is a typical case. All the villages within four and a half miles on each side of the road were assigned to work on different sections. Village elders and clan officers called the general clan meetings in their respective ancestral temples, to devise detailed schemes for managing this requisite work. On the walls of these temples were posted lists of working men chosen from each family; and the labourers so conscripted were sent out in turn to build the base of the road. During the work, their food was supplied by their respective clans. In case the clan fund was insufficient to meet this expense, additional assessment was made among all the families. For the work itself, however, not a single cash was paid. During the three years from 1930 to 1932, when the Ping-tan Road in Hwei-yang was being built, to every person regardless of age and sex was assigned the work of constructing eight feet of base. All of the children, many women who could not leave their homes, and many men who could not afford to leave their busy work in the fields had to pay 1 Yuan per capita for exemption from road building. Nearly 30 per cent of the peasant families involved in that conscription were unable to pay; hence some men of those families had to work for more than one assignment, and they worked from 8 o'clock in the morning till 6 in the evening. Perhaps as one of the worst examples of labour requisition for road building, reference may be made to the road built during the summer of 1933 from Nan-hsiung to Sin-fung (a district in Kiangsi). Here, each conscripted family had to work from four to fourteen days. In each case, the place of work was not determined by propinquity to the home, but was singularly decided upon by drawing lots. The clans in Nan-hsiung did not furnish food to the road builders who had to provide their own food. So the peasants had to carry their food and other belongings every day for a long distance, often ten miles. The present system of public road building has undoubtedly delivered a heavy blow to agricultural labour in Kwangtung; and in some cases, like the one just mentioned, it has been even worse than the military requisition of labour. There is a great lack of animal power in China, especially in the south; hence, whenever an army is on the march, military requisition forces numerous peasants to be transporters of supplies. It is said that in the hilly southwestern provinces, during troop movements for any long distance, two peasants are needed on the average for each soldier. Of course, those peasants taken by the requisition are hardly ever paid, but at least they do not have to provide their own food.

Besides the tax on labour power, there are plenty of other taxes on the cost of agricultural production. Just by way of illustration, mention may be made of the sales-levies recently imposed upon rice-chaff for feeding pigs, and bean-cake as fertilizer. While the price of the pig falls, the feed of the pig becomes more expensive because of the tax. In November, 1933, the peasants in the vicinity of Canton were unable to settle their accounts of rice-chaff even when the pigs were sold and the market price for them had been realized. Though meantime the price of bean-cake has dropped from 3.00 to 1.60 Yuan, no less than 0.50 of this 1.60 Yuan is tax. The bean-cakes bear a total burden of sales and transit taxes even higher than the import duties on foreign manufactured fertilizer. In the port of Swatow alone, the transit tax on bean-cake amounts to more than 1,000,000 Yuan a year.

Practically no single item of agricultural products escapes taxation. Not considering the auxiliary products of the farm, such as pigs, cows, ducks and chickens, all of which pay market or transit taxes, or both, but just taking the main agricultural product, the rice, let us see what a tax burden it has to bear. Again, there is no uniform tax rate among the different districts on rice, whether it is collected on sales or on transit. In the district of Chung-shan, where rice is the chief product, one-sixth of the price is tax; for, in January, 1934, according to the reports of rice mills in Shek-ki (the largest trading centre of Chung-shan), rice per picul had to bear a total tax burden of 1 Yuan when its average market price was 6 Yuan. In the vicinity of Kin-tu-wan, the popular rice shipping place in the 6th Ku of Chung-shan, the tax burden has been even higher. On top of a sales tax, an extra transit tax is levied. Approximately 800,000 piculs of unhusked rice, corresponding to 520,000 piculs of marketable rice, is estimated as the total production in the district. No less than 40 per cent of the unhusked rice is shipped to the neighbouring districts, and nearly one-third of this shipping goes through Kin-tu-wan, from which port a huge quantity is transported also to Shek-ki. Every year about 200,000 piculs of unhusked rice are shipped to Shek-ki and Kiang-men from Kin-tu-wan. In spite of the fact that the Provincial Bureau of Finance has recently issued an order to stop the transit tax on rice, it is still levied in a disguised form by the local authority. It happens that one of the close relatives of the district magistrate is the local police chief and concurrently the head of the land tax bureau. Wielding his full power as head of the marine police, he keeps away all steamers towing the rice ships except those hired by himself. Thus he is able to impose a monopolistic charge on rice transportation, namely double the commercial rate. In addition to this exorbitant charge which is really a very heavy transit tax, each ship towed must pay every time 4.60 Yuan demanded by an almost unthinkable tax, called "the ship-bow fee."

The tax rates on agricultural land also vary with the different districts. In Hwei-yan, the main tax per mow is only 0.38 Yuan, but with all the surtaxes and miscellaneous assessments, from 1.20 to 1.50 Yuan must be paid for every mow. There are about 1,300,000 mow of cultivated land in this district; in spite of several tens of specially appointed land tax collectors from the magistrate's office and two commissioners from each sub-district to urge this tax payment, the income from the land tax actually received by the Government is less than 90,000 Yuan, representing only 5 per cent of the expected return. This explains why Hwei-yang has been most talked about as a district where corruption and squeeze in connection with the land tax are rampant. However, similar conditions, though not quite so bad, are to be found in other districts as well.

Before 1912, the tax on the best land in Tai-shan was only 0.40 Yuan per mow; but now in the same locality, for 1 mow of the upper medium grade, one has to pay a land tax of 1.60 Yuan. The land tax in the northern part of Hoh-pu is generally 1.10 Yuan for each unit of cultivated land, which is about one-half of a mow; in the southern part, the tax is less, but at least 1.00 Yuan. On the average, the land tax in Hoh-pu is about 2.00 Yuan per mow. In Chao-an the main land tax is only 0.42 Yuan per mow; but with surtaxes for the police and for public road building, the total amount reaches 3.00 Yuan. Within the last three years (1931-1934), the rate of the land tax has increased twice in the district of Chung-shan, till today the total annual collection of land taxes has reached the sum of 7,000,000 Yuan. There are two kinds of agricultural land in Chung-shan: the fertile fields in the valley, called *Kang-tien*, and the still more fertile *Sha-tien* near the sea. For every mow of the former type, the main land tax is 0.24 Yuan, there is a fee for watchmen of 0.34 Yuan, and a sur-tax for the police of 0.60, thus making a total of 1.18 Yuan. Compared with this, however, the total amount of taxes for every mow of *Sha-tien* is almost three times as high. There are the main land tax of 0.24 Yuan, the *Sha-tien* sur-tax of 0.30, the watchmen's fee of 0.34, the sur-tax for police of 0.60, and the sur-tax for armed guards 1.75; in short, each mow of *Sha-tien* has to bear a tax burden of 3.23 Yuan. In the 9th Ku of Chung-shan, an additional assessment of 0.10 Yuan per mow has been made for building watch towers against the bandits.

As a rule, the tenants pay one half of the total amount directly to the tax collectors, the other half being paid by the landlord, but in addition they often have to make regular payments to the organized bandits. These payments to bandits are called the "black ticket fees." For, should a peasant family in the Sha-ku, nearly in every case a tenant, neglect to pay such fees, the bandits would issue a "black ticket" to prevent it from cultivating or from reaping the harvest. Thus every year, at the time of planting in March, the Sha-ku tenants have to pay 3.00 Yuan per mow to the bandit organization; and in July and in November, they have to pay for every mow the taxes amounting to 1.60 Yuan as well as the "black ticket fees" of 5.00 Yuan. The total tax burden per mow which is borne by the tenants is, therefore, no less than 9.60 Yuan. In some places where bandits have been driven away by the governmental troops, the "black ticket fees" are abolished only to make room for new extra assessments made by the military authority on the spot. This tax of 9.60 Yuan, to which must be added an unknown portion of the tax paid by the landlord and included by him in the rent of 15.00 Yuan per mow, brings the tenant's non-productive outgo to a total equalling four-fifths of his crop income of about 30.00 Yuan per mow.

In some other districts the land tax is just as high as in Chung-shan. In Kieh-yang, 9 Yuan is taxed for every mow. In Ying-teh, the main tax per unit of cultivated land is 1 Yuan, the sur-tax for land survey is 0.60 Yuan, and the sur-tax for road building 1.40 Yuan; and since every three and one-third units of cultivated land in Ying-teh equal the standard mow, the total amount of taxes per mow is nearly 10 Yuan. Perhaps the highest land tax is being collected in the district of Kao-yao, where the main tax is only 0.38 Yuan but with all the additional levies total up to 11 Yuan per mow. The land tax in the southwestern part of the province is comparatively lower; in Meu-ming, for instance, it is 1.50 Yuan per mow. But here it is also rising. The local land unit of Meu-ming is one-third of the standard mow. In 1932 the tax was 0.15 Yuan per unit, in 1933 it increased to 0.28 Yuan, and in 1934 it

INCREASE OF LAND TAX PER MOW
(Ten Representative Villages in the District of Pan-yu, 1928 and 1933)

Village	Amount of Tax per Mow	
	1928	1933
	Yuan	*Yuan*
Pei-tseng	0.50	0.80
Sha-dien-kang	0.40	0.90
Kang-sin	0.48	0.98
Nan-pu	0.40	1.00
Kiu-tseng	0.40	1.10
Mei-tien	0.60	1.25
Huang-pien	0.40	1.30
Tang-yai	0.40	1.40
Lung-tien	0.42	1.40
Ting-lung-fong	0.40	3.75
Average	0.44	1.39

reached 0.50 Yuan. Within the short period of three years, the land tax has been advanced to fully three times what it was in 1932.

The statistics for the ten representative villages of the district of Pan-yu show that in the course of five years the land tax there also trebled.

One of the ten villages listed opposite, Tang-yai, has had its land tax increased four times in seven years; for the rate of tax per mow in 1926 was 0.35 Yuan, in 1928 it was 0.40, and in 1933 it became 1.40. According to the present grain price in Tang-yai, the average crop income per mow is about 20 Yuan; thus the land tax would amount to 7 per cent of it. But in the case of Kao-yao, a district where the highest land tax is being levied, the percentage of tax to income is much greater. In this district the first harvest yields 400 catties per mow of unhusked rice, and the second yields 50 catties more. With the market price dropped to 5 Yuan per 100 catties, the total crop income per mow is only 42.50 Yuan; and the land tax of 11 Yuan, therefore, takes 26 per cent thereof.

CHAPTER VI

TRADE AND CREDIT

UNDER THE heavy and double burden of tax and rent, many peasants can partly rely upon the remittances they receive from their emigrated relatives, but by far the majority of them have nothing to live upon except what they produce. The remittances from overseas have been rapidly decreasing within the last four years both in individual size and in the aggregate. There used to be a time, especially in 1931, when a hundred million Yuan were sent home in a year through the three cities of Hong Kong, Canton, and Swatow. This total was reduced by 1934 to one third and possibly one fifth of its former amount. In Chung-shan the total annual remittance used to amount to more than 30 million Yuan, was still about 20 million in 1931, but melted to 2 million Yuan in 1933. It is said that the district of Tai-shan has received a total remittance of 40 million in 1930; but three years later this sum had shrunk to about seven-tenths of that size. Most of the money sent back to Chung-shan and Tai-shan has been from the Americas, while most of that received in Mei-hsien and Chao-an has come from Siam, Singapore, and other regions to the South. (Usually the inclusive term *Nan Yang* or South Seas is used to designate the Netherlands-Indies, the British Colonies in South East Asia, French Indo-China, the Philippines, and Siam. Sometimes Burma and India also are included, but there are much too few Chinese residents in those countries). It seems that the decline of remittances from the Americas has been more rapid than that from other places of migration. Yet, what is received in Mei-hsien has been reduced by three-fifths within the last four years. In the village of Ning-hu, in the southern part of Chao-an, a renowned place for South Sea emigrants, the annual remittance once totalled 200,000 Yuan; but in 1933 it was only 40,000 Yuan. One reason is that emigrants are returning constantly and in great numbers, another that agricultural exports to the South Sea regions are declining rapidly. While tax and rent are the old two-edged axe which cuts into the life tree of the peasants, the present unemployment and economic depression are a new and equally sharp axe which cuts into it at the same time. The peasants, therefore, in selling their products, are under even greater pressure than they were a few years ago; their keener competition brings down the price further, and consequently forces them to sell more of their product at a ruinous price.

The annual shipment of mandarin oranges from one village named Hou-tsao, in the southern part of Chao-an, used to be valued at more than 300,000 Yuan, three-tenths of it destined for the Shanghai market and seven-tenths for the South Seas. The business depression of recent years, however, has caused the price of orange seedlings to drop from 30 to 6 Yuan per 100 pieces, and there must have been a similar fall in the price of oranges. In 1934, the prices of the oranges, bananas and sugar cane for direct consumption shipped from this village dropped off by 40 to 50 per cent compared with those of the preceding year. It is no wonder that many orchard peasants of Pan-yu, Tung-kwan, and Tseng-cheng have gone into bankruptcy. In the Sha-ku of these districts, the cost per mow producing the same kind of cane has been estimated at 280 Yuan, including 20 to 30 as rent; and the income per mow has been decreasing from 400 or 500 Yuan to little over 60 in 1933.

In Chung-shan it is estimated that only when the price of unhusked rice per picul is 6 Yuan or more can a rent of 10 Yuan per mow be paid. Up to recent years, when the rice mills of Shek-ki collected the rice from each new harvest, 7 Yuan per picul was paid. But the price dropped so rapidly that in the spring of 1934 even the best grade of unhusked rice was marketed for 4.20 Yuan per picul. Similar conditions exist in the southwestern part of the province. In the beginning of 1934, the average price per picul in the district of Meu-ming was not more than 4 Yuan, which was just about one-half of the price prevailing the preceding year. The rice produced in Meu-ming and its neighbouring districts is mostly shipped through Shui-tung. The market price per picul in this port was 11 Yuan between 1928 and 1932 and 7 Yuan in the beginning of 1933; but it dropped to 5.50 Yuan in the autumn of that same year. Shui-tung used to send out 400,000 Yuan worth of rice every year; the total export of 1933, however, brought in only 100,000 Yuan. The market price in the interior is usually lower than it is at the port. During the two years of 1932 and 1933, the price per picul of unhusked rice in Lien-kiang was 6 Yuan, 14 per cent lower than in Shui-tung. It has also been dropping, till now it is 3.50 Yuan.

With the decline of the price of rice, the prices of taro, potato, carrots, and peanuts have also gone down. From the North River Valley great quantities of taro and peanuts are transported southward to various cities of the delta region; but recently the prices have fallen to a level which barely covers the transportation charges. Within the last five years, the price of unhusked rice in Pan-yu has been cut by 36 per cent; and during the same period the prices of peanuts, taro, and potato have been cut by 15 per cent, 25 per cent, and 50 per cent, respectively. (See table 24).

The prices of various products which in the peasant economy are of an auxiliary nature have met with equally if not more drastic reductions. Take for instance the market price of pigs in Canton. It was 34 Taels per picul in the beginning of 1933, 28 Taels in September, 24 Taels in October, 20 Taels in November, and by the end of that year it was only 15 Taels. (The Tael is from 20 to 30 per cent more than the Yuan). Of course, similar reductions of the price have taken place in all the pig-raising districts of the province. The annual total shipment of pigs from Shui-tung to Kiang-men has been valued at 2,600,000 Yuan, but it is now estimated as worth only 800,000 Yuan. Likewise, the annual total of chickens sent out from Meu-ming has been reduced from more than 600,000 Yuan in value to less than one-half of this within the last three years. In Shun-teh and Nan-hai, where many peasants have to dump their silkworms into fish ponds, the fishes have been well nourished, but their market prices are also declining. From between 25 and 30 Yuan per picul the fish prices in these districts have fallen to from 12 to 18 Yuan. The income from fish used to be auxiliary to that of mulberry and cocoons, but now it looms in the mind of the peasant as his last hope of making ends meet. The sudden drop of fish prices cannot but shatter this last hope of his; and facing these lively creatures in the pond, he knows not how to cry, nor how to laugh.

Under the pressure of rent, tax and debt, the peasant has to sell, anyhow, no matter what the price. To sell is not enough, he has to borrow. He runs to the pawnbroker or the money lender not only for a loan to make possible the cultivation of his holding, but often also for something with which to maintain his family while the crop grows.

Where can he get a loan? Presumably he has already exhausted whatever credit facilities his own family and circle of friends afford. So long as he has something to pawn, he will not even go to the clan elders unless his clan has special arrangement, which is rare now-a-days, for loans at a low interest rate to the rank and file of the membership. Like the poor of all countries, he goes to the pawnshop because it is the most convenient source of relief for his particular woe. The pawnshop involves no irksome negotiations, and the risk in dealing with it is limited; there is no question of his right to his original property when he can pay the debt and the interest charge within the agreed term. The pawnshop in Kwang-tung is a private business but usually organized as a collective venture of several families. Municipal or other non-profit-making pawnshops are extremely rare in China.

If the would-be borrower has nothing to pawn, he is likely to go first to his own landlord or, if that gentleman is an absentee, his agent. If landlord or agent are in the business in a big way, he usually will not want to bother with a small loan and curtly send the tenant on his way. In that case our friend, now getting more anxious, will visit a merchant, a rich peasant, or some other land-lord or landlord's agent whom he knows to be in the business of lending money. Nearly all the small landlords are, in fact, money lenders. With the merchants, money lending is more distinctly a sideline, and a smaller proportion go in for this kind of business. Rich peasants only occasionally accommodate a tenant farmer, and few of them make a serious business of lending. As between these three classes, the would-be borrower has no very definite preference, as a rule: although the risk he takes with them may take different forms, there is little to choose between them, and he will be guided by his contacts or by what he knows about them personally. In the case of the rich peasant he may eventually have to work off his debt if he cannot pay it. In that of the merchant he may be forced to purchase from the lender at exorbitant prices and, in case he cannot pay, have to sell his crop to him at the lender's valuation. In the case of the landlord-lender, the risk is greatest of being deliberately led into a snare, so as to lose what little land he owns; for this type of Shylock not only wants his pound of flesh, but is usually interested in making a loan only when he sees a chance of adding to his property, that is when the borrower is willing to stake his land in guarantee.

It is estimated that, of the indebted peasant families in Kwang-tung, three-tenths have borrowed because of sickness, funeral, wedding, or the expense of some other unexpected occasion; but seven-tenths have borrowed solely to obtain food for their families, which usually consists of taro, potato, and other edibles that are cheaper than rice. Broadly speaking, two-thirds of the peasant families in Kwangtung are under a debt of some sort. Because of particular difficulties involved in investigating indebtedness, the statistical result of such study often shows a percentage lower than what it really is.

Although a few of these debts may represent temporary or permanent loans for current farm business purposes, most of them must be regarded as signifying the existence of a temporary or permanent insolvency. In the ten representative villages of the district of Pan-yu, 44 per cent of all the village families and 53 per cent of the peasant families are indebted in this sense. (See table 25). In the fifteen villages of Hwa-hsien, just north of Pan-yu, 63 per cent of all the peasant families are indebted (see also table 25). The result of investigation by correspondence in sixty-seven villages in Pan-yu shows a much higher percentage of indebtedness. Of these sixty-seven villages, 5 have 60 per cent of the peasant families in debt, 9 have 70 per cent, 16 have 80 per cent, 4 have 85 per cent, 18 have 90 per cent; and nearly all the peasant families in three of the villages of southern Pan-yu are in debt. In other words, out of a total of 67 villages, 50 have 70 or more than 70 per cent of their peasant families in debt.

In the famous silk district of Shun-teh, some 70 per cent of the peasant families are in debt. Perhaps this is typical of all the districts on the Pearl River Delta. In the East River Valley, the indebted peasant families are 50 per cent in Hsing-ning, 60 per cent in Wu-hwa and Lung-chwan, 65 per cent in Hwei-lai, 70 per cent in Ping-yuen, 80 per cent in Chiao-ling, and 85 per cent in Lung-men. The percentages for the districts in the North River Valley are 60 for Lien-hsien and Kuh-kiang, and 80 for Loh-chang, Yang-shan, Ju-yuen, Ying-teh, and Wung-yuen. In the southwestern corner of Kwangtung are the four contiguous districts of Hwa-hsien, Sin-i, Tien-peh, and Meu-ming; and the correspondence from a hundred villages distributed in these districts shows that more than one-half of the villages have more than 60 per cent of the peasant families in debt. What is more remarkable is the fact that one-fourth of all these villages have an indebtedness involving more than 90 per cent of the peasant families.

Usually in winter the peasants borrow grain for paying rent, or food for their own consumption; and in spring, at the time of sowing rice, they borrow cash. But the tendency of recent years indicates clearly that the debt is increasingly in the form of money. In the villages of Kwangtung generally, the monthly interest on a cash loan is from 2 to 3 per cent, and the annual interest is about 20 per cent. Many districts, however, demand higher rates of interest. It is 4 or 5 per cent a month in most of the districts of Hainan Island; and it is 5 per cent a month in many villages of Hwa-hsien, Meu-ming, Ta-pu, Kieh-yang, and Kao-ming. In Meu-ming, when a cash loan is of less than 20 Yuan, the monthly interest rate is nearly always 5 per cent. In the Sha-ku of Pan-yu, a monthly interest of from 4 to 6 per cent is demanded. Again, in many places of the province the annual interest is above 20 per cent. For instance, 30 per cent is found in Ying-teh, 40 per cent and 60 per cent are found in Sin-hwei, 70 per cent is found in Sin-i; and in the village of Lai-tseng, in Wu-chwan, as much as 100 per cent is being charged.

The usual interest charged on a loan in grain is 30 per cent for six months. Of course, in many cases a much higher rate is demanded; the figures given in the table on page 90 may serve as examples:

INTEREST RATES ON LOANS IN GRAIN

District	Village	Semi-annual Rate
		Per Cent
Ling-shui	Kwang-lang	50
Wu-chwan	Yin-ti	60
Tien-peh	Kiu-hsui-miao	60
Wu-hwa	Tin-yun-tung-ko	60
Yun-fou	Au-yuan-kien	80
Kuh-kiang	Ma-yang	50
Loh-chang	Lu-yai	50
Sin-i	Cha-shan	70
Meu-ming	Yue-lien-tang	70
Sin-hsing	Peh-kiu-tung-yai	100
En-ping	Ta-heng	100
Tai-shan	Hu-lu-shan	100

The charge is highest when grain is paid, because the principal and interest of a cash loan are paid in grain, for, in that case the borrower is exposed to manipulations, against his interest, of price and weighing. This form of usury is found in almost every district; the creditor is said to be "cultivating a flower in grain," while in this same process the debtor is said to be "selling away the green seedlings" in advance. Landlords, merchants, or rich peasants rent out their money to the peasants in need and demand grain from them immediately after the harvest; the amount of grain needed to pay off principal and interest is agreed in advance when, in his dire necessity, the borrower knowingly lets himself in for a total charge which may amount to as much as 200 per cent. This is not, however, a fixed interest rate but a total arrived at in devious ways. The lender, to begin with, has the right to interpret the market price of the grain at the time the loan is made; it is he who measures the grain when it is delivered, and who determines its grade. Herein lies a huge profit, a fully blossomed "flower" which is "cultivated" in the short period of six months or less.

Just opposite the city of Ko-chow, perhaps two miles from its western gate, there is a village named Si-nga, administratively belonging to the 4th Ku of Meu-ming. Many peasant families in this village sell away their green crops in advance; this is locally known as *Mai-ti-hwei,* meaning perhaps the advanced selling of rice stalks which otherwise might be reserved for making potassium fertilizer. When they borrow 1 Yuan of cash, four months later they have to pay four-tenths of a picul of unhusked rice. The market price of this quantity is rarely below 2 Yuan. In the northern part of the province, such as in the districts of Loh-chang and Yang-shan, the usurers begin their "cultivation of the grain flower" at the end of the third month of the lunar calendar, and this "grain flower" is picked before the end of the sixth month. Here, within a quarter of a year, the peasants have to pay a debt of 3 Yuan with 1 picul of rice valued at 5 Yuan.

In many places the rate of interest is still rising. Take the wealthy silk district of Shun-teh; here the peasants used to have a sort of financial arrangement for mutual help;, only a comparatively few have gone to the usurers. In recent years, when the silk and cocoon industry collapsed, they had to resort to borrowing at an exorbitant rate of interest. A semi-annual interest is imposed upon the debtor even when he pays back all the money within two or three months. And any unpaid debt beyond half a year must bear a compound interest, under the burden of which the indebted peasants can hardly ever redeem themselves. In Tien-peh and in Meu-ming, there are villages where within the last five years the rates of interest have generally gone up by 10 per cent; in some other places of Sin-i they have gone up by 20 per cent; and in not a few villages in the districts of Ying-teh and Mei-hsien, during that same period, by 40 per cent.

These increases in interest rates reflect the general impoverishment of the districts named, that is, an increased demand, and, in the circumstances, urgent need for money. They also reflect a growing insecurity which has driven money out of agricultural enterprise and out of the rural region into the cities and into permanent investment. Five years ago, a monthly interest of eight-tenths of one per cent has been very common among the villages near Kwang-hai, in southern Tai-shan; but with the decrease of remittances from overseas, the monthly interest rate increased correspondingly, until it is now 2 per cent. Whenever the clan organization is under the control of a few greedy and corrupt officers, rent accumulations furnish a sure basis for clan usury. Loans from the clan are usually for one year; but when the interest is not in default, payment of the principal may be postponed. Should the interest in default be equal to the principal, however, the property of the debtor is taken away to cover the total debt. Should his own property be insufficient to realize this purpose, then the property of his relatives is taken away also (see above, page 36). In this connection, should these relatives attempt to refuse, then they are driven out of the clan; and after that anybody communicating with them is punished. The grant of a large clan loan, just like a lease of clan land, is often made in a single contract; and the borrower of the loan fund as a whole, divides the asset into smaller parcels and makes a profit on that sub-division. The price for the original privilege often is a matter of bidding. The one who offers the highest interest secures the bid.

There are three well known private institutions for money-lending: the Tang, the An, and the Ya. They are all pawnshops, but the time limit for redeeming the pawns is different with each of them. The Tang usually commands a larger capital; it can afford to sustain a longer rhythm of capital circulation, and there-fore sets up a time limit of three years. With smaller capitaliza-tions, the An and the Ya fix the terms at two years and one respectively. Because of the increasing tax burden and the ever growing difficulties in disposing of the unredeemed pawns, many of the Tangs, and in a lesser degree the Ans, have recently gone out of business. In the city of Chao-chow, the business centre of Chao-an, there were 103 Tangs in 1826; there were still 40 in 1897; but now there remains only 1 Tang in the whole city, tottering and struggling for its existence. The Tangs and the Ans which carry on business today manage to do so either by greatly under-assessing the value of the pawn, or by greatly in-creasing the rate of interest. The usual monthly interest rate has been from 2 to 3 per cent; but now it has become much higher in many places. In Kwang-chau-wan, for instance, the monthly interest of Tang is 6 per cent.

Meantime, the institution of Ya is spreading all over the province. The interest rate of the Ya is so high and the time limit is so short that it would be difficult to find a parallel else-where. In Kwang-ning, a very productive district of bamboo and lumber, many landlords have recently opened shops of Ya. For a pawn worth 10 Yuan, only 2 or 3 Yuan is paid by the shop; the time limit for redeeming is usually one of six months and sometimes even shorter; and the interest must be paid twice a month at a monthly rate of from 10 to 20 per cent. Perhaps the largest number of any one kind of pawns taken in by the Ya is that of bare cotton quilts, filthy, old, and hard pressed. Many peasants have to pawn their agricultural implements: the hoe, the rake, the harrow, and the plough. These pawns so dear to the peasants are piling up in the aisles of the store rooms of the Ya. Liu Siu-ting, the chairman of the Chamber of Commerce in Wung-yuen, who is concurrently the owner of a big Ya called Kwang-an, has spoken of the fact that in his shop agricultural implements have multiplied three times within the last four years.

Evidently, there is a limit to what may be pawned by the peasants, and that is why, when these people are too poor, usury itself cannot flourish. To continue rural exploitation, usury capital must work hand in glove with its twin brother, trade capital. In Kwangtung, numerous dealers of unhusked rice, of fruit, of sugar, and of pigs, extort from the peasantry a huge profit through both price and interest. Where tax and rent are paid in advance, such as in the Sha-ku, the peasants easily fall victims to the joint pressure of trade and usury capital. The peasants are often prevented from planting or harvesting when their rent or tax is in default. They are compelled to borrow from the rice dealers with their crop as security. The unhusked rice itself is for paying the debt, and the amount to pay is determined by a price dictated by the dealers. The borrowing is done in the end of the fifth month of the lunar calendar; the harvesting takes place in the beginning of the sixth; and the debt is to be paid at the latest at the end of that harvest month. Nominally, the loan is for two months, with a monthly interest of 3 per cent; but actually it is paid in one month with 6 per cent of interest.

Still more calculating and complicated is the usury practice of the big dealers of sugar cane (for direct consumption) in Canton. They also can most readily extend loans to the peasants, who usually cultivate such cane to the extent of three or four mow per family, for which at least 300 or 400 Yuan are needed as expenditure. The major part of such a loan, however, is not in cash. At the time of planting, the dealers give seedlings to the peasants.

One or two months later, and for a second time in the autumn, they furnish fertilizer in the form of peanut-cake. They furnish also the bamboo supporters for canes during the windy season. They lend money to the peasants only on the occasions of paying rent. All the non-cash loans are figured out by a price usually 10 per cent more than on the market. Nominally the loans are for eight months at a monthly interest of 1½ per cent; but actually they are paid in four months with 3 per cent of interest. Furthermore, upon "selling" cane to the dealers, the peasants have to pay a commission of from 3 to 8 per cent and also some miscellaneous charges amounting to 2 per cent; the creditors always demand these from the peasants, even if the cane is being "sold" to some other dealer. Hence the debtor peasants have to "sell" the product of their labour to their creditor dealers, who often deliberately mark the best quality for lower grades. With such diverse ways of exploitation, the cane growers pay an interest rate amounting to more than 6 per cent per month.

Similar practices of usury are found in Chao-an, especially in the villages where mandarin oranges grow. Loans are granted usually two or three years ahead of the fruit yielding; the fruit is valued at one-half of the market price; thus, nominally the monthly interest is only 1 or 2 per cent; but actually from 5 to 6 per cent has to be paid. The big dealers at Swatow have found a close and powerful ally in a group of landlords and gentry in those orange-producing localities. They have undertaken a joint enterprise of exploitation, in which usually the latter furnish 20 per cent of the capital and the former 80 per cent. This group of landlords and gentry which is in business relations with the rich Swatow merchants, is known in Chao-an as *Two-chiao,* meaning the leading families. In the pig-producing district of Meu-ming, the joint operation of trade and usury capital has been going on for even more years than in the orange-producing districts. The pig dealers, the creditors, take in pigs from the debtor peasants at one-half of the market price. After the debt is deducted, the peasant should receive the balance; but he cannot receive it till the dealer himself has sold the pig.

The peasant in Kwangtung runs to the bosom of the usurer as a child might run to his grandmother, asking for a favour, helpless and naive. He runs to him not only with his agricultural products such as rice seedlings, unhusked rice, mulberries and cocoons, pigs and cows, and fruit of all kinds as securities, but also often with his daily necessities, like clothing, furniture, and the house in which he lives. In every village, there are always several families pawning out their agricultural implements. In almost every district there is the pawning as well as selling of children. Throughout the province an immense number of domestic semi-slave girls as well as licensed and unlicensed prostitutes, and a vast reserve of both, are simply helpless and mute victims on the altar of usury. In the southwestern part of Kwang-tung, where a peasant girl of ten years of age is sold for only 40 Yuan, a big landlord family sometimes keeps as many as twenty such peasant girls. Some of them are given to the daughter of the house at the time of her marriage, as a part of the dowry.

Only as a last stand in their desperate struggle, do the owner peasants resort to mortgaging their land. Personal properties can be replaced, more children can be bred; but land is hard to get back once it has been lost. The typical Chinese peasant holds on to the land after the last quilt has gone to the pawnbroker. In a Western country the farmer is not afraid, as a rule, of a mortgage on his land if he should happen to own it; he regards it, rather, as an asset which enables him to put an amount of capital into his farm business which it would be difficult for him to secure as cheaply in any other way; and in case of need, the mortgage actually facilitates the sale of his land. But when a poor peasant in China mortgages his bit of land, he has practically no hope of ever getting it back. Everything conspires against him in his frantic effort to meet the interest charge, and eventually he loses not only the land but also this additional fruit of his labour. If he only knew, he would be far better off by selling outright at the start. Of course, intellectually he does know; but such is the emotional attachment of the peasant to his clod of soil that he will not look at the matter in an objective way. Like a person dying of a malignant disease who clings to life, he deceives himself to the last into hoping that his lot will not be like that of other men.

Sometimes one-half of the peasant families have mortgaged their lands, as in many villages of Wung-yuen and Mei-hsien, where the percentage of landowning peasants is relatively high. The mortgage price is from 50 to 60 per cent of the land price; very rarely is 80 or 90 per cent. Of course, only a very few peasants would like to sell their lands; most of them prefer to mortgage in the hope of recovering them. But once the peasants have stepped into the sepulchre of usury, they are led to descend down the inescapable staircase with only a remote chance of coming out again. At least 70 or 80 per cent of the landless peasants in Kwangtung have lost some of their land possessions through mortgage. According to the statistics of ten representative villages in the district of Pan-yu, the peasants there have mortgaged and sold 5 per cent of their land area within five years. (See table 26). In the village of Lung-tseng, in the 2nd Ku of Chao-an, no less than 3 per cent of all the peasant families have lost their land during the year 1933. Usury certainly wields an almost omnipotent power over those miserable producers with small means of production. Like a certain parasitic germ it seems to live in the capillary system of the small peasants, sucking the blood and weakening the heart, and forcing them to undertake agricultural production under more and more pathetic and pathological conditions.

CHAPTER VII

THE DECLINE OF WAGES AND THE LOSS
OF LABOUR POWER

HAVING seen how the ownership of agricultural lands is distributed, how the use of them is limited, and how the producers are exploited in various forms, we now should ask whether production itself is going upward or downward, whether the future for agriculture in this part of the world is growing brighter or gloomier. So far, no scientific and statistical data can be given to show the exact degree of decline in agricultural production, because no such investigation has yet been made in Kwangtung; but in the case of *Kwei-kwan* or large farms in the Pan-yu district, we know that the amount of unhusked rice produced per mow has been reduced from six to four piculs within the last thirty years. In the districts of Kao-yao, Wung-yuen, and Mei-hsien, the peasants in many a village told the writer that there had been decline in production even within the past ten years. With the exception of some vegetable gardens in the villages near Swatow, Canton, and Shek-ki, we may say that in general there has been no improvement or development in the practice of agriculture. Under these circumstances, the emigration going abroad and the rural exodus in general, the increasing prevalence of woman labourers in agriculture, and especially the decrease in agricultural wages which, as we shall see, is sure proof of the lowering of the standard of living among the peasantry, all reflect the discouragement and even loss of labour power.

Rapid concentration in land ownership and the consequent proletariatisation of the workers and contraction of the cultivated area per family have caused an increase in the number of unemployed peasants and a fall of agricultural wages. When the land cultivated by one family cannot absorb all the labour power of that family, some of the members will want to be employed in some other occupation or to sell their labour power. In the ten villages of Pan-yu investigated, 17 per cent of the working people from 840 families have to leave their homes for work. All those who are hired by the year, and no less than 68 per cent of those who are hired by the day, are working for rich peasants. Only 15 per cent of the day labourers are employed by poor peasants. (See table 27). While the poor peasants hire less than the equivalent of five days of labour per family, or less than one per mow, the rich peasants hire one labourer per family by the year and in addition 99 days of labour. On the land cultivated by the rich peasants, almost every mow has to employ labour for four days. (See table 28). Those rich peasants who cultivate not rice but even more commercialized crops, such as fruit, have to hire more workers, both for the year and for the day. (See table 29). When agricultural prices fall, the rich peasants have to reduce their costs of production; consequently they cannot afford to pay a wage as high as before. This accounts for the decrease of wages as well as the decrease of labour employed.

In most of the villages on the Pearl River Delta and the Han River Delta, agricultural wages are paid in cash; but in many villages of the southwestern part of the province, the day labourers as well as some of the year labourers are paid by a certain amount of grain, entirely without cash. In not a few places in Kwangtung, the agricultural labourers are receiving a mixed form of wage, consisting of both grain and money. From what may be figured out of the correspondence from 265 villages in 49 districts, no less than one-fourth of the villages still practice wage payment in kind. The wages both in kind and in money are falling off. For instance, the customary daily wage in many of the Meu-ming villages used to be from 0.40 to 0.50 Yuan, but it is now only between 0.20 to 0.30 Yuan. In the villages near Kwang-hai in southern Tai-shan, the daily agricultural wage for men has dropped in four years, 1930-1934, from 1.20 to 0.80 Yuan. In four years also, 1929-1933, the daily wage paid for work during ordinary seasons in Tang-yai, a village very near Canton, has dropped from 0.60 to 0.40 Yuan, while that for the busy harvesting season has dropped from 1.80 to 0.80 Yuan. Just in one year, 1932-1933, the wage of the year-labourer in Tien-peh district has been reduced from 14 to 10 piculs of unhusked rice, and that in Sin-i from 11 to 8 piculs.

The wage in kind has never been high. In Hwei-yang, Teh-king, En-ping, Meu-ming, Sin-i, Tien-peh, and some other nearby districts, an agricultural labourer hired by the year used to receive from 2 to 20 piculs of unhusked rice in addition to his board and various other perquisites. (The range of wages for the individual districts is, of course, less wide and represents different degrees of experience). When the market price of unhusked rice stood at 6 Yuan per picul, in 1932-1933, the total annual wage earnings of labourers varied between 12 and 120 Yuan. But during the following winter, when the price fell off by 42 per cent, that is, from 6 to 3.50 Yuan per picul, the annual wage-earnings of these labourers dropped to a range of from 7 to 70 Yuan.

In a pre-capitalistic society, wages in general are not only lower than in the capitalistic, but they have a far greater variation of scale owing to the lack of an articulated and unified market for labour power. There is, thus, a wide variation of wage scales among the districts and even among nearby villages. Often, within the area of a few miles, wages in kind vary by 100 per cent, with even greater differences between various hsien. The same can be said of wages in cash. Take, for instance, a group of villages in the northern part of Pan-yu; the annual wage of an agricultural labourer is 80 Yuan in the village of Huang-pien, 100 in Yun-pien, 120 in Hoh-pien, and 130 in Peng-pien. All these villages are from one to one and a half miles from Chia-ho, a rural marketing centre.

A comparision between the land price and the income of an agricultural labourer shows the relative ease or hardship for him when he desires to acquire a piece of land. This may not be as good an index of the adequacy of a wage rate as is the respective cost of living in the regions for which such a comparison is ventured. But, quite apart from the difficulty of securing adequate data on the cost of living of rural families on a sufficient scale to make generalizations reliable, actually the conditions in different countries vary too much to make such comparisons significant. For example, differences in climate affect all the major requirements of subsistence, while differences in political systems determine what part of the standard of living is provided for from public funds. A comparison, in so far as it is practicable, of wages in relation to the price of land in various regions has the advantage that it deals with a value which every agricultural labourer desires to purchase if he can, and which in itself is an economic index of another sort.

In the district of Chitoor, in the southern part of India, an agricultural holding as large as one mow costs as little as four Yuan. In Bikol, in southern Luzon, one mow of the best rice land costs 16 Yuan. Of all the agricultural lands in the United States of America, those in Iowa are usually considered the most valuable; and in Iowa the land price was highest in 1920; yet one mow of land in Iowa was only 85 Yuan in that year. In North China one mow has an average price of below 100 Yuan; in Kwangtung the price is decidedly much higher, running up to 500 or 600 Yuan per mow in several districts. But as the wages in this province are at the same time far below the scale of those in America, the hope for an agricultural labourer to get a piece of land is still more remote. Let us examine the statistics opposite of a number of villages of Pan-yu, and we shall see that, though the year labourer is furnished with lodging and food by his employer, his annual cash income is below the price of one mow of the medium-grade land. After the hard work of an entire year, he often receives only one-half of that land price.

In other districts of Kwangtung, the wages of agricultural labourers are equally low. The statistics for the fifteen districts listed on page 102 may serve as fair examples.

In the valley of West River, the annual cash income of an agricultural year-labourer is sometimes only one-third of the price of one mow of medium-grade land. In the district of Yuh-nan, for instance, the wage is 40 Yuan, but the land price is 120. The wage is sometimes only one-fourth of the land price, such as in Hoh-shan, where the usual wage is 50 but the usual land price is

AGRICULTURAL WAGES IN PAN-YU

Village	Wage of Year-Labourer	Usual Price of Medium-Grade Land
	Yuan	Yuan per Mow
Mei-tien	70	80
Wu-lung-kang	50	90
Chang-sha-pu	90	100
Hsieh-chia-chuan	70	80
Pei-tang-hsiang	50	60
Ya-kang	70	100
San-kang-hsiang	70	80
Pan-hu	50	70
Mo-chian	80	150
Tang-yai	120	150
Kang-sin	90	140
Tseng-pien	100	150
Chi-sha	100	180
Tu-hwa	120	150
Kong-hwei	120	200
Heng-yuen	70	100
Sha-tsun	60	80
Li-ko	160	270
Chi-sha-hsiang	100	160
Yun-ning	80	160
Tan-shan-hsiang	70	180
Ke-tseng	100	230
Shih-chi-hsiang	50	120
Kiu-pi	90	200
Pei-shan	150	300
Lun-tu	120	240
Kong-tseng	90	200
Chien-tze	80	200
Tso-kao-wei	120	300

200 Yuan. In Kao-yao the wage is still lower; the usual cash income for a year-labourer is about 40 Yuan, the usual price of a mow of medium-grade land is 300 Yuan. In the upper region of the East River wages are just as low. The usual annual wage in Hwo-ping is 20 Yuan, while the usual land price is 80; the wage in Hsing-ning is usually one-fifth of the land price, the former being 40 and the latter 200 Yuan.

AGRICULTURAL WAGES IN KWANGTUNG

District	Usual Wage of Year-Labourer	Usual Price of Medium-Grade Land
	Yuan	Yuan per Mow
Hwei-yang	60	100
Tung-kwang	70	80
Ping-yuen	50	60
Lung-chwan	60	70
Mei-hsien	200	400
Wu-hwa	60	150
Teh-king	40	70
Yun-fou	65	130
Tai-shan	70	200
Chung-shan	150	300*
Yang-kiang	100	200
Yang-chun	60	80
Fuh-kang	40	60
Wung-yuen	35	100˙
Ying-teh	50	120

With the exceptions of Yang-kiang and Yang-chun, very low agricultural wages prevail in the whole south-west of Kwangtung, as may be seen from the following table.

AGRICULTURAL WAGES IN FIVE SOUTHWESTERN DISTRICTS

District	Usual Wage of Year-Labourer	Usual Price of Medium-Grade Land
	Yuan	Yuan per Mow
Lien-kiang	30	70
Wu-chwan	40	120
Sin-i	30	90
Hwa-hsien	30	100
Lo-ting	40	150

In many villages of southwestern Kwangtung, a year-labourer receives only 20 Yuan; and when it is paid in the form of unhusked rice he does not get more than 25 Yuan in value. In Montana,

---

* Kong-tien.

where wages are relatively high and land prices relatively low, three days' wage earnings may equal the land price of one mow; in Canada, particularly in the wheat region, it may take five days' wage to make this equivalence. In Iowa it requires the wage of about 24 days to earn the necessary amount; in India or in the Philippines that of about two months. In the Yellow River Valley an agricultural year-labourer must accumulate his wage earnings for two or three years to purchase one mow of land of medium grade. But in Kwangtung, the southernmost part of China, a strong agricultural labourer, in the prime of his life, must not spend anything for himself or for his family out of his cash wage, but must accumulate, not merely for one, two, or three years, but sometimes for seven or eight years all of his money income, in order to be able to acquire one mow of the medium-grade land.

To acquire one mow, however, does not help him much. At least from five to seven mow for rice cultivation are necessary, as we have seen, to maintain a peasant family at the subsistence level. In the village of Feng-tseng, in the 5th Ku of Meu-ming, one mow of medium-grade land not so long ago has cost 360 Yuan; only in recent years has it dropped to 150 Yuan. Yet, here the annual agricultural wage is not more than 20 Yuan. It takes the total wages of seven years to equal the price of one mow. In the village of Cho-tseng, in the second Ku of the same district, the price of one mow of medium-grade land used to be 450 Yuan; it has now dropped to 240. But the wage of a year-labourer in this village is only 30 Yuan, one-eighth of the price of one mow.

One of the surest proofs that a condition exists in which agricultural production is discouraged is an abnormal proportion of female labour in the total labour power applied to the land—and this even in regions where field work by women is customary. As the more mobile part of the labouring population, it is the men who first come out from under an intolerable burden, either by engaging in some other form of labour if such can be found or by migrating. When rural employers increase the proportion of women labourers, this is a sign that male labour has become scarcer or less docile or sufficiently less efficient to make the employment of women preferable. An increased employment of women may also reflect a desperate general economic situation in which a peasant woman who normally works for her own family is forced to seek employment for wages—even though the wages offered may not suffice to support even her alone.

The prevalence of woman labour in the villages of Kwangtung has, in the main, this last-named cause. There are probably few women, if any, who are engaged for work on the land by the year other than those permanently attached to the employer's household and living with it, doing of course many other tasks besides. But it is a significant fact that throughout the province women out-number men among the day-labourers in agriculture. This is not, perhaps, quite as dramatic a proof of abnormal conditions as it might appear to Western readers, since in the rice-growing regions of the Orient female field workers are always more numerous in proportion than they are in the West. Nevertheless, to have more women than men engaged in agricultural day-labour is certainly unusual.

The work of female labourers is less productive than that of male; and the wage is correspondingly lower if for no other reason. According to figures obtained for the ten representative villages in the district of Pan-yu, women earn on an average only three-fifths of what men earn; and this proportion does not vary much as between ordinary times and especially busy seasons. (See table 30). Almost the same proportion results from a comparison of figures given in letters from 52 villages in Pan-yu where no special statistical study was made; here, it appears, the average daily wage for women is one of 0.26 Yuan, and that for men one of 0.45 Yuan. Taking the province as a whole, there is considerable variation in this proportion, as also in the actual wage rates for men and women, as will be seen in the table on page 105.

The relatively high wage for both men and women in Tai-shan and Sin-hwei is explained with the large number of emigrants who have gone from these districts to the United States and, to a lesser extent, to the colonial dependencies of Western powers. For these emigrants have long sent remittances to their families which made them independent or, at least, less dependent on wage labour. Returned emigrants employ more labour, and especially also more domestic labour; hence women's wages in these districts are also proportionately higher than elsewhere in relation to men's wages. There is, however, an even more potent effect of earnings and savings overseas on the wages of agricultural labour: as we have

AVERAGE WAGE OF AGRICULTURAL DAY LABOURERS IN ORDINARY SEASONS

District	Men	Women	
	Yuan	Yuan	Per cent of Men's Wage
East River			
Hwei-yang	0.30	0.20	67
Mei-hsien	0.59	0.37	62
Chiao-ling	0.37	0.25	67
West River			
Kao-yao	0.60	0.40	67
Tai-shan	0.80	0.56	70
Sin-hwei	0.95	0.65	68
Pan-yu	0.45	0.26	58
North River			
Ying-teh	0.29	0.20	68
Wung-yuen	0.30	0.15	50
Loh-chang	0.36	0.23	64
South-western			
Lo-ting	0.26	0.12	46
Sin-i	0.17	0.06	40
Kin-hsien	0.35	0.25	71
Fang-cheng	0.20	0.10	50

seen in an earlier chapter, many of the emigrants, whether still abroad or returned, put their money into agricultural land, thus raising prices and the cost of living. With these higher costs, the demand for labour also goes up, since they call for a use of the soil that will yield a higher return—unless the land is taken out of cultivation altogether because, even with increased output, it is no longer possible to meet the charges upon it. Under this special influence, therefore, a rising wage standard and a shrinkage of the cultivated area have in parts of this region at times occurred simultaneously.

As in the case of labourers employed by the year, the wage is lowest also for day labourers in the south-western part of the province. The extremely low wages mentioned for some districts in the above table rest on no typist's error. In many villages of Tien-peh the wage for women is even less than 0.06 Yuan. In the district of Meu-ming and in some districts of Hainan Island, such as Ting-an, Lin-kao and Ling-shui, there are villages where male and female day labourers alike receive no wage at all but are glad to get work for two square meals a day.

It is interesting to note that in Mei-hsien, whence a majority of the young men have emigrated to the countries of the south (the *Nan Yang*), and where women have taken the place of men as the major source of labour power in agriculture, the wage of a day-labourer is much less than it is in Tai-shan or in Sin-hwei.

The origin of this unusual prevalence of female labour goes back a long time and is described in the chronicles of Mei-hsien—edited during the reign of Kuang Hsu (1875-1908), vol. VIII, pp. 53-55. This mountainous district swarmed with migrants from more northern parts of China at the end of the thirteenth century, and again in the middle of the seventeenth. We read:

"These political and war refugees found that the fertility of the land did not suffice to support them all. Hence some of the men acquired the habit of pursuing trade in distant places, and women were left behind to attend to the work in the fields as well as that of their homes. Ever since the beginning of foreign trade, in modern times, the people of Mei-hsien have flocked to various regions in the Southern Seas. At first they hired themselves out to work in different capacities. When they had accumulated the savings of years, they became independent traders. Most of them visited their homes about once every ten or fifteen years, many of them once every five or seven years; but none returned within three years. There were cases of emigrants who had left as small boys and came back for the first time when they were bald-headed elders. Some of them left their wives behind; some of them left their betrothed behind, and these, because of their poverty, had to come unwed to the homes of their prospective father-in-law. Unmarried daughters and daughters-in-law did most of the work in the kitchen, in the vegetable garden, in the orchard, in the woods, and in the rice fields."

Now-a-days, if one were to walk along the highway leading from the West Gate of Mei-hsien to the neighbouring district of Hsing-ning, one would meet group after group of women carrying on their shoulder-poles coal from the third Ku, or tea and dried persimmons from the second Ku. Leaving the highway and climbing up into the hills, one would still meet line after line of female transport workers, toiling up and down the steep and rocky paths with heavy loads of lump coal and lime stone. These women are anything from ten to fifty years of age; and for a whole day's work of carrying their loads over ten miles of hilly land they receive a daily wage of 0.60 Yuan. Because of the large demand for female labour in this region, their wage is relatively high. Even for field work the pay of women here is as high as 0.40 Yuan—a mere pittance, of course, yet wealth compared with the earnings in regions with fewer labour opportunities.

Where female labour predominates, productivity suffers. Busy with their inescapable home work, women labourers often have no time to plough in the interval between two crops. So one may see field after field of sparsely planted green wheat shooting up between the yellow stubble of the previous rice crop. According to the unanimous opinion of village elders in Mei-hsien, women are not physically capable of deep ploughing which is needed if two good crops are to be obtained in one year. The prevalence of woman labour in the upper regions of East River and North River thus has created a serious loss of production.

In the lower region of the East River, too, woman labour is very common in agriculture. This is especially true in Hwei-yang where almost one-half of the day labourers are women and where the average wage is correspondingly low.

Until recent years, there have been very few women agricultural labourers in the lower region of the Han River, in the districts of Kieh-yang, Chao-an, and Cheng-hai. The economic depression of the last few years, however, has brought about a very apparent depreciation of labour power: the traveller notices the unusually large number of women who carry water in the streets; and women are also seen more often than in the past working for wages in the fields.

In the lower region of West River, female agricultural labour is a familiar phenomenon. In only twenty of the seventy-two villages investigated in the districts of Pan-yu, women do not participate in field work; in all the others men and women work together in agriculture. In fact, in some of the villages of northern Pan-yu—Pan-hu, Ya-hu, and others of that neighbourhood— whence many men have emigrated to Canada and Cuba, there is a situation similar to that in Mei-hsien: more women than men are engaged in agriculture.

We are here concerned only, of course, with women who go out to work in agriculture at a daily wage, not with the vast number of peasant women who, year in and year out, work on their husband's or family's farm at whatever job most needs their help. This phenomenon of a large proportion of woman day labourers in agriculture is probably unique. Taking the 261 villages in 46 of the districts investigated by correspondence alone, we find that in less than one-third of the villages—75—no women work as agricultural labourers; in fifteen of the villages it is reported that women have become the majority of wage workers in agriculture; and in six of the villages practically all the agricultural work is carried on by women. Although a large proportion of woman labour is customary in all the south-western provinces of China, it is remarkable that Kwangtung, with its relatively high productivity, cannot to a larger extent utilize the more productive labour of men.

For an explanation we have to go back to those factors in the social structure which, as we have seen, determine the primary relations in regard to the land and the conditions under which productive labour is carried on. These relations do not, in Kwangtung, warrant a full employment of male labour on the land. This is, of course, irrefutably proved by the statistics of occupations and of migration. For example, taking again the ten representative villages in the district of Pan-yu which have been intensively studied, we find that in more than one-half of the peasant families at least one member is working at something else as his chief means of adding to the household's livelihood—usually as a coolie, pedlar, or shopkeeper—or has enlisted as a soldier. (See table 31). As one would expect, the proportion of families with such auxiliary sources of income is greatest among the poor peasants. Because their children have no opportunity of receiving an education, less than 2 per cent of these families have members engaged in one of the"professions"—among which, in the Chinese village, one must reckon not only those familiar in the Western world but also letter writers, fortune tellers, geomancers, and others who live primarily by the exercise of trained mental abilities. While the richer peasants occasionally engage in trade, and the landlords have open to them possibilities of official appointments as well, there are almost no opportunities left in the village to the poorer peasants and their sons when crops fail, or prices drop, or for some other reason work on the land can no longer support the whole family. Too often, they not only have to move away; but even when they settle in some other locality they have to adopt some new mode of living. Thus, it has been possible to ascertain that of 82 families which have moved away from the ten representative villages in the district of Pan-yu in the twenty years ending in 1933—there is no reason to doubt that this is a representative sample—only about 30 per cent have remained in agricultural work; in the other cases the chief breadwinners have become coolies, soldiers, pedlars, and shopkeepers. (See table 35).

There is practically no mention of industrial employment in the reports which the home villages receive of these men. The mills and factories of Shanghai, the most industrialized town in China, cannot absorb more than a fraction of the bankrupted peasants and their sons who beg for work at their doors. With their much smaller industrial development, the towns of Kwangtung, even Canton itself, offer even proportionately to population much fewer chances of such employment.

So far, there has been no systematic investigation of the peasant exodus in this province. The familiar emigration figures include, of course, only part of the movement from the villages and give no clue to the social composition of the emigrant population— though it is well known that most of them are of the peasant class. To get a sense of the relief afforded to purely agricultural districts by overseas migration, one would have to secure detailed figures for specific areas. Observations in a few districts must here suffice. Of the total population of Kai-ping, about one-tenth has gone overseas in the life time of the present generation. We learn that more than ten thousand live in the South Seas countries and twice as many in the Americas. More than twenty thousand of the inhabitants of Sze-hwei have gone abroad, most of them to Singapore from where, no doubt, they have distributed themselves over Malaya and the nearer parts of Sumatra. No less than three hundred thousand Tai-shan people are still said to be living abroad, although the district itself almost seems to be over-flowing with returned emigrants and their families. According to the Federation of Returned Emigrants in Tai-shan, 35 per cent of the emigrants are in the South Seas area, 25 per cent in the United States, 20 per cent in Canada, 8 per cent in Australia, and 12 per cent in other foreign countries.

The districts of North River have a smaller proportion of their sons living abroad; but the outward movement of the population is pronounced. Take Wung-yuen, for instance. This is a purely agricultural district where even the usual rural handicrafts are not much developed. In the last five years, its population has decreased by one-fifth, from 150,000 to 120,000—and this in spite of the barriers to Chinese immigration almost everywhere.

During the past twenty years, at least 5 per cent of the population of Hwei-yang have left the district to become soldiers or coolies. In the eighth Ku of Heri-yang alone, one-tenth of all the peasants go to Hong Kong every year as seasonal labourers. Hsing-ning and Mei-hsien have sent forth swarms of pedlars and small retail traders. Fully two-thirds of the migrants from Mei-hsien are in business, and some seven-tenths of them have gone in that capacity to the Netherlands Indies. According to statistics compiled by the District Government at the end of 1931, one-half of the people in Mei-hsien are engaged in agriculture; and as many as 22 per cent of the total working population are employed outside of the district:

POPULATION OF MEI-HSIEN IN 1931

	Men	Women
Residents		
Native-born	171,912	205,819
Immigrant	4,650	1,198
Emigrants	83,235	25,845

In the lower region of Han River, the proportion of emigrants is just as high, apparently, though only approximate figures are available. According to local officials, there ought to be about two thousand young men in Ning-hu, a village in the sixth Ku of Chao-an, but eight hundred of these have gone abroad. In the village of Hwa-mai, in the seventh Ku, as many as seven-tenths of the young men have gone overseas. It is said that one out of every five men born in Chao-an has sailed to the South Seas.

While a good deal of attention has been given to the matter of overseas migration, much less is known about the apparently enormous loss of productive labour through enlistment. Yet, more men leave the villages of south-western Kwangtung to enlist in the army than leave to emigrate. To illustrate: nearly four out of every five of the men in the 19th Route Army, which has become famous through its part in the defence of Shanghai in 1932, have been peasants from Kwangtung—about 10 per cent of them from the North River, 30 per cent from the East River, and Han River regions, and no less than 60 per cent from the south-western part of the province. At present, though the majority of the higher officers in the Kwangtung troops are from the East River districts, the largest percentage of enlisted men is from the districts of the south-west.

It is apparently very difficult, with the lack of general population data, to estimate the number of people who constitute the continuous outward movement from the villages. But it is generally agreed that because of the decline of agricultural prices and wages, and partly also because of extensive road-building with its serious addition to the tax burden and that of compulsory labour, the drain of rural workers has increased during the five years 1928-1933. In the eastern part of the province, as in Mei-hsien and Chiao-ling, annual emigration has probably risen by 35 per cent; in the southwestern part, as in Sin-i, Meu-ming, and Tien-peh, probably by 30 per cent; and in the middle part, as in Teh-king, Shun-teh, Pan-yu, Chung-shan, and Tai-shan, probably by 20 per cent.

Since the middle of the nineteenth century, the capitalistic development of the Malaysian colonies and of the western part of North America has virtually used up at least one million Kwangtung peasants by means of a labour recruitment which, especially in its earlier stages, fell little short of a disguised form of slave trade. Although in recent years the world economic depression has forced many of the descendants of these emigrants back to China, British Malaya and the Netherlands East Indies have, since 1934, opened their doors again to a tiny slit—especially by encouraging the immigration of Kwangtung women. Female labourers are admitted to these colonies not only free of the tax required for male immigrants; but in some cases a 50 per cent contribution toward their steamer passage is paid by labour agents for prospective employers. Apparently, this cheaper labour power is invited by rubber manufacturers to bring the trade out of its depressed condition by means of lower production costs. There is also a larger migration than in the past of women and children who join emigrant husbands and fathers overseas. While formerly even the least successful of Kwangtung emigrants in these near-by countries of the *Nan Yang* expected sooner or later to re-join his family in the home village, the desperate condition of agriculture in that province no longer permits of such hopes for many of them. In consequence, no longer looking forward to a return for permanent residence, Kwangtung emigrants in growing numbers decide to bring their wives and children over to wherever they are and to make their permanent homes there.

The rubber manufacturers of Malaya are by no means the only people who appreciate the rich reservoir of cheap labour offered by Kwangtung. The cheapness of that labour, especially of women, is indeed, appalling. From such villages as Shun-teh, Pan-yu, Chung-shan, and Sin-hwei, nearly twenty thousand peasant girls have been taken to Hong Kong and are now working as housemaids with the status of a *mui-tsai*. Other streams of peasant girls, bought and sold, move toward the cities of the province itself. In Swatow, the market price of a housemaid used to be about 100 Yuan (see also pp. 60 and 61), and that of a concubine about three times more; but at the present time, with the increased inability of the peasants to support their daughters, the average price may be said to be from 30 to 40 per cent lower. There was a time when military officers of the lower ranks made lavish purchases of peasant girls. Now the purchasing power of these circles, too, and of other urban classes is diminished; and a far greater number of peasant girls are being pawned rather than sold outright. The price obtained by pawning is, of course, much lower than obtained by sale; but since the peasant father is often not in a position to redeem the pledge, pawning often simply represents a disguised form of selling at much less than the customary price.

We close our survey, then, upon a note of misery beyond which human experience can hardly go except in times of catastrophe. For the purpose of the present study, however, we may look upon the cheapness of life and labour in Kwangtung merely as proof that whatever internal mechanisms there are in the structure of its agricultural society to adjust population to a lessened remunerativeness do not suffice under present conditions. Nor can these conditions be looked upon as a passing phase which will make

way for recovery as world trade revives and with it the demand
for Chinese agricultural products. The loss of labour power to the
region here under review is not in the nature of an overflow, a
surplus resulting from too fast a growth of population, as it might
have been some generations ago. It diminishes production and
impoverishes the land just as surely as do the exhaustion of the soil
and the decay of the improvements on which the ancestors have
toiled. For, land and labour are inescapably linked. In the past,
the rulers of China and their provincial administrators knew that
a certain minimum of well-being among the peasants is as essential
to productivity and, consequently, to rich tax returns as are the
keeping up of irrigation works and dykes, and the renewal of the
soil's fertility. That knowledge has not been lost; but there has
been a change in the distribution of power, and new factors in the
social relations which govern agricultural production have altered
the economic foundations. Labour power in Kwangtung today
is neither utilized effectively nor treated as an export commodity:
it is simply wasted, and this under conditions of utmost misery
and degradation. The region has become an area of capitalistic
exploitation without experiencing a corresponding development of
its resources, physical and human. The economic apparatus has
not been adapted to the changing requirements brought about by
the closer dependence of local economies upon world currents; it
has simply been permitted to break up. There has been no
re-organization of the relations between the producing and the
non-producing participants in the economic process, but merely a
scramble in which not even the most elementary precautions were
adopted to keep alive the goose that lays the golden egg. This
scramble has, of course, its political side. But, as we have seen,
cause and effect must here be clearly discerned. For example, the
tax authorities can no longer prevent the destruction of the tax
sources by exorbitant landlords. And even the most honest and
conscientious local officials cannot protect oppressed peasants
against the exactions of hired gangs.

The present study is not intended to provide conclusive proof of
any theory. It is, rather, a slice of contemporary life which the
student may examine for himself. Within the limited scope of
this survey it has not been possible to obtain all relevant information. There is room, and indeed need, for many further studies.

But it is hoped that enough of the facts have been presented here to give the thoughtful inquirer clues to the essential problems.

APPENDIX

TABLE I

PEASANT FAMILIES OF 152 VILLAGES IN 38 DISTRICTS OF THE
PROVINCE OF KWANGTUNG.

District	Number of Villages	Number of Families	Number of Peasant Families			
			Owners (a)	Tenants (b)	Agricultural Labourers (c)	Total
Ying-teh	8	474	142	278	37	457
Hwei-yang	2	185	88	71	3	162
Hsing-ning	1	200	140	60	—	200
Mei-hsien	2	275	183	80	12	275
Chiao-ling	2	265	102	138	25	265
Tien-peh	15	602	137	281	52	470
Sin-i	6	648	126	339	79	544
Meu-ming	43	3,191	884	1,639	242	2,765
Yang-kiang	2	129	70	22	16	108
Yun-fou	2	100	20	80	—	100
Lo-ting	3	2,900	1,070	720	405	2,195
Sin-hsing	1	30	10	20	—	30
Kao-yao	2	1,550	485	545	240	1,270
Teh-king	2	290	120	110	50	280

(a) Peasants most or all of whose holdings are owned by their families.
(b) Peasants who lease all or most of the land they cultivate.
(c) Peasants who depend on wages as the principal source of livelihood.

APPENDIX

District	Number of Villages	Number of Families	Number of Peasant Families			
			Owners (a)	Tenants (b)	Agricultural Labourers (c)	Total
Hoh-shan	1	1,500	100	1,300	—	1,400
Shun-teh	5	3,150	295	1,983	300	2,578
Chung-shan	6	1,875	435	1,009	61	1,505
Tai-shan	12	1,224	224	737	63	1,024
Wu-chwan	2	137	73	20	25	118
Tan-hsien	1	100	100	—	—	100
Kiung-tung	1	50	40	7	3	50
Cheng-mai	1	100	60	6	4	70
Ting-an	1	145	75	30	30	135
Lin-kao	1	380	260	80	40	380
Loh-hwei	1	115	95	12	3	110
Kiung-shan	1	50	49	1	—	50
Hwa-hsien	7	859	113	482	69	664
Kuh-kiang	3	798	161	377	60	598
Wung-yuen	2	870	182	472	116	770
Nan-hsiung	1	42	10	25	7	42
Jen-hwa	2	116	9	101	6	116
Wu-hwa	2	175	42	89	10	141
Ping-yuen	1	550	120	320	10	450

(a) Peasants most or all of whose holdings are owned by their families.
(b) Peasants who lease all or most of the land they cultivate.
(c) Peasants who depend on wages as the principal source of livelihood.

District	Number of Villages	Number of Families	Number of Peasant Families			
			Owners (a)	Tenants (b)	Agricultural Labourers (c)	Total
Loh-chang	4	427	249	122	17	388
Ju-yuen	1	125	12	102	11	125
Lien-hsien	1	600	420	85	35	540
Kai-ping	1	224	112	80	5	197
Kwang-ning	3	325	27	190	108	325
Total of 38 Districts	152	24,776	6,840	12,013	2,144	20,997
Per Cent of Different Peasant Families			32.6%	57.2%	10.2%	100%
Per Cent of Peasant Families to the Total of Village Families			84.7%			

(a) Peasants most or all of whose holdings are owned by their families.
(b) Peasants who lease all or most of the land they cultivate.
(c) Peasants who depend on wages as the principal source of livelihood.

TABLE 2A

PEASANT FAMILIES IN SIXTY-NINE VILLAGES IN THE DISTRICT OF PAN-YU

Village	Total Number of Families in Village	Number of Peasant Families			
		Owners	Tenants	Agricultural Labourers	Total
Nan-pu	150	8	95	2	105
Shen-shan	450	22	406	—	428
Lo-chi	160	—	150	—	150
La-ya-kang	770	—	462	—	462
Yang-mei-kang	72	—	13	—	13

APPENDIX

Village	Total Number of Families in Village	Number of Peasant Families			
		Owners	Tenants	Agricultural Labourers	Total
Siang-kang	130	8	96	—	104
Huang-pien	108	21	53	20	94
Yun-pien	93	—	88	—	88
Yuen-tseng	45	15	20	5	40
Hoh-pien	150	10	78	12	100
Peng-pien	200	25	105	50	180
Pei-shan	140	20	58	6	84
Chi-sha	256	14	210	22	246
Tu-hwa	300	30	240	30	300
Lung-tu	300	40	100	140	280
Sia-chu	420	88	235	13	336
Lung-tien	70	5	44	—	49
Cho-kao-hwei	57	10	30	6	46
Sung-pei-kang	26	2	22	—	24
Sung-kang	27	—	27	—	27
Chien-tse	50	30	10	2	42
Kong-tseng	300	200(a)	90	10	300
Kong-pu	100	8	80	6	94
Heng-yuen	200	4	115	1	120
Kiu-tseng	137	25	60	—	85

(a) These families have some orchard lands near their houses, only 3 or 4 of them have rice fields.

118

APPENDIX

Village	Total Number of Families in Village	Number of Peasant Families			
		Owners	Tenants	Agricultural Labourers	Total
San-meng	350	30	250	20	300
Yo-chi	300	10	50	—	60
Tang-shan	800	144	331	5	480
Ling-pien	350	74	171	—	245
Kang-sin	70	—	53	—	53
Hwa-lung	600	25	295	30	350
Shan-ou	75	—	16	—	16
Tseng-pien	200	8	167	5	180
Mei-shan	88	5	80	—	85
Sha-tien-kang	119	7	105	2	114
Pei-sha-tang	230	3	212	—	215
Ta-pu-ta	70	—	70	—	70
Lo-tseng	160	5	149	—	154
Hsieh-chia-chwan	240	20	200	—	220
Si-yuen-tseng	62	5	45	12	62
Mei-tien	170	16	121	8	145
Wu-lung-kang	280	28	168	84	280
Chang-sha-pu	130	20	100	10	130
Chang-kang	85	2	28	10	40
Tsun-chi-yuen	22	1	18	3	22
Sha-tsun	716	50	333	257	640

APPENDIX

Village	Total Number of Families in Village	Number of Peasant Families			
		Owners	Tenants	Agricultural Labourers	Total
Shi-chi	2,400	300	600	300	1,200
Pang-kiang	1,100	33	363	264	660
Sin-chia	750	10	430	160	600
Lung-hsian	1,500	15	1,308	147	1,470
Kwei-tien	127	96	18	6	120
Ka-tseng	254	45	161	20	226
Kin-pu-tu	60	14	37	3	54
Kiang-pei	105	10	60	10	80
Li-ko	1,400	40	896	184	1,120
Kong-tei	450	60	168	52	280
Siu-kong	200	30	100	20	150
Tang-yai	110	8	75	15	98
Pei-tseng	400	40	320	40	400
Peng-hu	4,065	—	3,590	10	3,600
Yuan-yai	300	30	210	30	270
Pei-tang	140	13	110	7	130
·Chi-shan	1,300	100	350	50	500
Mo-chiang	243	80	80	20	180
Tsun-ko	370	—	360	—	360
Kiup-pi	42	—	27	15	42
Song-kang	436	80	260	10	350

Village	Total Number of Families in Village	Number of Peasant Families			
		Owners	Tenants	Agricultural Labourers	Total
Shi-ma	1,121	390	515	70	975
Yu-lung-chwan	270	104	156	—	260
Total of 67 Villages	26,971	2,536	16,043	2,204	20,810
Per Cent of Different Peasant Families		12.0%	77.4%	10.6%	100%

Per Cent of Peasant Families to the Total of Village Families   77.2%

TABLE 2B
PEASANT FAMILIES IN TWENTY-TWO VILLAGES IN THE DISTRICT OF HWA-HSIEN

Village	Total Number of Families in Village	Number of Peasant Families			
		Owners	Tenants	Agricultural Labourers	Total
S-Sian	216	17	136	17	170
Shu-ling	350	100	200	—	300
Chu-kao-pu	120	—	60	—	60
Siao-pu-li	330	3	294	3	300
Ping-shan-liang	205	28	112	20	160
Li-pei	300	48	192	—	240
Yang-O-tseng	1,000	140	490	70	700
San-chi	400	30	240	30	300
Siao-tung-fu	200	30	120	—	150
Ma-chi	620	120	330	—	450

Village	Total Number of Families in Village	Number of Peasant Families			
		Owners	Tenants	Agricul-tural Labourers	Total
Huang-chi-shan	680	100	280	—	380
Chu-tseng	220	40	120	—	160
Tien-mei	880	198	475	119	792
Wen-den-kien	250	—	148	37	185
San-hwa	1,380	331	773	—	1,104
Ya-wu	450	121	284	—	405
Long-tu	600	72	468	—	540
Shi-ku(a)	800	40	160	—	200
Sho-kiang-tang	475	213	214	—	427
Lian-tang	600	50	400	50	500
Sin-chuan	45	5	40	—	45
Kuan-Lo-pu	200	30	120	—	150
Total	10,321	1,716	5,656	346	7,718
Per Cent of Different Peasant Families		22.2	73.3	4.5	100%

(a) 600 out of these 800 families are half-merchants and half-peasants.

TABLE 3
PROPORTION OF LANDLESS PEASANT FAMILIES
(Ten Representative Villages in the District of Pan-yu, 1933)

Villages	Total Peasant Families	Landless Peasant Families			Per Cent. of Landless in Total of Peasant Families
		Agricul-tural Labourers	Tenants	Total	
Nei-tien	148	10	97	107	72.3

Villages	Total Peasant Families	Landless Peasant Families			Per Cent. of Landless in Total of Peasant Families
		Agricultural Labourers	Tenants	Total	
Nan-pu	105	0	70	70	66.7
Ting-lung-fong	87	16	36	52	59.8
Sha-tien-pang	114	2	64	66	57.9
Pei-shan	73	10	29	39	53.4
Kwei-tien	60	10	18	28	46.7
Lung-tien	95	20	23	43	45.3
Kang-sin	52	7	14	21	40.4
Kin-tseng	105	4	26	30	28.6
Huang-pien	84	4	20	24	28.6
Total	923	83	397	480	52.0

TABLE 4

LANDLESS FAMILIES AMONG DIFFERENT PEASANT CLASSES

(Ten Representative Villages in the District of Pan-yu, 1928 and 1933)

Peasant Class(a)	Total Number of Families		Landless Families		Per Cent. of Landless Families to the Total	
	1928	1933	1928	1933	1928	1933
Rich	109	107	20	19	18.3	17.8
Middle	202	193	58	52	28.7	26.9

(a) As more fully explained in the text, p. 8, for present purposes "middle peasants" are those whose holding corresponds to the minimum of land area which if owned suffices to support a family of average size for the village if planted to the usual major crop of that village. A "poor" family is one whose land holding is below this potential income—the income from auxiliary sources normally being negligible. A "rich" family is one whose land holding at least equals that of the minimum and which employs either one or more labourers all the year around or a number of day labourers in seasonal work exceeding the average employed by middle peasants in that village.

Peasant Class(a)	Total Number of Families		Landless Families		Per Cent. of Landless Families to the Total	
	1928	1933	1928	1933	1928	1933
Poor	493	540	286	326	58.0	60.4
Agricultural Labourers	82	83	82	83	100.0	100.0
Total	886	923	446	480	50.3	52.0

TABLE 5

COMPARISON OF OWNER AND TENANT FAMILIES AMONG DIFFERENT

PEASANT CLASSES

(Ten Representative Villages in the District of Pan-yu, 1928 and 1933)

Peasant Class	Owner Families		Per Cent		Tenant Families		Per Cent	
	1928	1933	1928	1933	1928	1933	1928	1933
Rich	55	57	50.5	53.3	54	50	49.5	46.7
Middle	75	75	37.1	38.9	127	118	62.9	61.1
Poor	116	117	23.5	21.7	377	423	76.5	78.3
Total	246	249	30.6	29.6	558	591	69.4	70.4

TABLE 6

COMPARISON OF OWNED AND LEASED LANDS FARMED BY DIFFERENT

PEASANT CLASSES

(Ten Representative Villages in the District of Pan-yu, 1928 and 1933)

Peasant Class	Number of Mow Owned		Per Cent		Number of Mow Leased		Per Cent	
	1928	1933	1928	1933	1928	1933	1928	1933
Rich	1,182.2	1,115.5	40.8	40.8	1,712.1	1,617.5	59.2	59.2
Middle	748.5	673.0	30.3	29.7	1,719.5	1,594.3	69.7	70.3

Peasant Class	Number of Mow Owned		Per Cent		Number of Mow Leased		Per Cent	
	1928	1933	1928	1933	1928	1933	1928	1933
Poor	509.8	525.0	18.1	17.2	2,306.2	2,530.7	81.9	82.8
Total	2,440.5	2,313.5	29.8	28.7	5,737.8	5,742.5	70.2	71.3

TABLE 7
COMPARISON OF OWNED AND LEASED LANDS FARMED BY DIFFERENT
PEASANT CLASSES
(Eight Representative Villages(a) in the District of Pan-yu, 1928 and 1933)

Peasant Class	Number of Mow Owned		Per Cent		Number of Mow Leased		Per Cent	
	1928	1933	1928	1933	1928	1933	1928	1933
Rich	1,043.2	958.8	38.3	37.9	1,679.1	1,570.0	61.7	62.1
Middle	665.6	603.1	28.3	27.8	1,682.7	1,567.2	71.7	72.2
Poor	415.1	436.2	16.1	15.5	2,167.0	2,387.1	83.9	84.5
Total	2,123.9	1,998.1	27.8	26.6	5,528.8	5,524.3	72.2	73.4

(a) Lung-tien and Kwei-tien excluded.

TABLE 8
LEASED LANDS FARMED BY DIFFERENT PEASANT CLASSES
(In the Villages of Kang-sin and Kiu-tseng, 1933)

Peasant Class	Irrigated		Non-irrigated	
	Mow	Per Cent	Mow	Per Cent
Rich	37.0	35.6	67.0	64.4
Middle	240.5	68.5	110.8	31.5
Poor	316.3	60.2	209.2	39.8
Total	593.8	60.5	387.0	39.5

TABLE 9
LAND OWNED BY DIFFERENT PEASANT CLASSES
(Ten Representative Villages in the District of Pan-yu, 1933)

Peasant Class	Number of Families	Mow Owned	Per Cent of Families	Per Cent of Mow Owned
Agricultural Labourers	83	—	9.0	—
Poor	540	540.5	58.5	22.1
Middle	193	689.8	20.9	28.3
Rich	107	1,212.0	11.6	49.6
Total	923	2,442.3	100.0	100.0

TABLE 10
LAND POSSESSIONS IN DIFFERENT SIZES OF HOLDINGS
(Ten Representative Villages in the District of Pan-yu, 1933)

Peasant Class		Mow 0	Mow 0.1—5.0	Mow 5.1—10.0	Mow 10.1—20.0	Mow 20.1—30.0	Mow 30.1—50.0	Above 50 Mow	Total
Rich	Families	19	27	27	17	8	5	4	107
	Per Cent	17.8	25.2	25.2	15.9	7.5	4.7	3.7	100.0
Middle	Families	52	96	35	10	—	—	—	193
	Per Cent	27.0	49.7	18.1	5.2	—	—	—	100.0
Poor	Families	326	193	18	3	—	—	—	540
	Per Cent	60.4	35.7	3.3	0.6	—	—	—	100.0
Agricultural Labourers	Families	83	—	—	—	—	—	—	83
	Per Cent	100.0	—	—	—	—	—	—	100.0
Total	Families	480	316	80	30	8	5	4	923
	Per Cent	52.0	34.2	8.7	3.3	0.9	0.5	0.4	100.0

APPENDIX

TABLE 11
AVERAGE NUMBER OF MOW OWNED PER FAMILY AMONG DIFFERENT PEASANT CLASSES
(Ten Representative Villages in the District of Pan-yu, 1933)

Peasant Class	Mow Owned	Families	Average Mow per Family
Poor peasants and Agricultural Labourers(*a*)	540.5	623	0.87
Middle	689.8	193	3.57
Rich	1,212.0	107	11.33
Total	2,442.3	923	2.65

(*a*) In this table poor peasants and agricultural labourers are classed together, although as seen in the previous tables the labourers' families own no land, on the principle that in demonstrating the average land possession for the different classes, the labourers are to be classed with others of the poor peasants who have no longer any land of their own.

TABLE 12
DECREASE IN AVERAGE NUMBER OF MOW OWNED
(Ten Representative Villages in the District of Pan-yu, 1928 and 1933)

Peasant Class	Average Mow Owned per Famly		Index for (1928 = 100) 1933
	1928	1933	
Poor Peasant and Agricultural Labourers (*a*)	0.91	0.87	95.6
Middle	3.79	3.57	94.2
Rich	11.83	11.33	95.8

(*a*) See note, table 11.

TABLE 13
TOTAL AREA OF LAND CULTIVATED BY DIFFERENT PEASANT CLASSES
(Ten Representative Villages in the District of Pan-yu, 1933)

Peasant Class	Families		Mow Cultivated	
	Number	Per Cent	Number	Per Cent
Poor	540	64.3	3,055.7	37.9

Peasant Class	Families		Mow Cultivated	
	Number	Per Cent	Number	Per Cent
Middle	193	23.0	2,267.3	28.2
Rich	107	12.7	2,733.0	33.9
Total	840	100.0	8,056.0	100.0

TABLE 14
NUMBER AND PROPORTION OF LAND HOLDINGS OF DIFFERENT SIZES CULTIVATED
BY DIFFERENT PEASANT CLASSES
(Ten Representative Villages in the District of Pan-yu, 1933)

Peasant Class		Mow 0.1—5.0	Mow 5.1—10.0	Mow 10.1—20.0	Mow 20.1—30.0	Mow 30.1—50.0	Mow 50.1—100.0	Above 100 Mow	Total
Rich	Families	8	21	26	24	18	8	2	107
	Per Cent	7.5	19.6	24.3	22.4	16.8	7.5	1.9	100.0
Middle	Families	36	66	71	16	4	—	—	193
	Per Cent	18.6	34.2	36.8	8.3	2.1	—	—	100.0
Poor	Families	320	156	53	8	3	—	—	540
	Per Cent	59.3	28.9	9.8	1.5	0.5	—	—	100.0
Total	Families	364	243	150	48	25	8	2	840
	Per Cent	43.3	28.9	17.9	5.7	3.0	1.0	0.2	100.0

TABLE 15
AVERAGE NUMBER OF MOW CULTIVATED PER FAMILY AMONG DIFFERENT
PEASANT CLASSES
(Ten Representative Villages in the District of Pan-yu, 1933)

Peasant Class	Mow Cultivated	Families	Average Mow Per Family
Poor	3,055.7	540	5.7

Peasant Class	Mow Cultivated	Families	Average Mow Per Family
Middle	2,267.3	193	11.7
Rich	2,733.0	107	25.5
Total	8,056.0	840	9.6

TABLE 16
AREA DEVOTED TO CHIEF AGRICULTURAL PRODUCTS IN DIFFERENT VILLAGES
(Ten Representative Villages in the District of Pan-yu, 1933)

Village	Rice		Wheat, Cotton, Taro & Peanuts		Fruits		Vegetables	
	Mow	Per Cent	Mow	Per Cent	Mow	Per Cent	Mow	Per Cent
Nan-pu	1,378.4	98.9	15.0	1.1	—	—	—	—
Mei-tien	864.8	77.4	250.9	22.5	—	—	1.0	0.1
Ting-lung-fong	488.5	76.9	135.0	21.2	—	—	12.0	1.9
Sha-dien-kong	875.9	74.3	289.2	24.5	—	—	14.5	1.2
Kiu-tseng	709.9	66.6	340.0	31.9	0.6	0.1	15.4	1.4
Huang-pien	395.6	63.1	63.9	10.2	125.3	20.0	41.7	6.7
Kwei-tien	95.5	46.3	12.2	5.8	15.7	7.6	83.1	40.3
Kang-sin	176.6	40.6	251.5	57.9	1.4	0.3	5.0	1.2
Pei-shan	404.8	37.8	—	—	665.5	62.2	—	—
Lung-tien	89.8	27.5	—	—	237.3	72.5	—	—
Total	5,479.8	68.0	1,357.7	16.9	1,045.8	13.0	172.7	2.1

APPENDIX

TABLE 17
AREA DEVOTED TO CHIEF AGRICULTURAL PRODUCTS AMONG DIFFERENT PEASANT CLASSES
(Ten Representative Villages in the District of Pan-yu, 1933)

Peasant Class	Mow Culti-vated	Rice		Wheat, Cotton, Taro & Peanuts		Fruits		Vegetables	
		Mow	Per Cent	Mow	Per Cent	Mow	Per Cent	Mow	Per Cent
Rich	2,733.0	1,788.0	65.4	234.1	8.6	672.4	24.6	38.5	1.4
Middle	2,267.3	1,599.9	70.6	446.1	19.7	182.0	8.0	39.1	1.7
Poor	3,055.7	2,091.9	68.4	677.3	22.2	191.4	6.3	95.1	3.1
Total	8,056.0	5,479.8	68.0	1,357.7	16.9	1,045.8	13.0	172.7	2.1

TABLE 18
AVERAGE NUMBER OF MOW OWNED PER PERSON AMONG DIFFERENT PEASANT CLASSES
(Ten Representative Villages in the District of Pan-yu, 1933)

Peasant Class	Mow Owned	Number of Persons	Average Mow Per Person
Poor Peasants and Agricul-tural Labourers(*a*)	540.5	2,928	0.18
Middle	689.8	944	0.73
Rich	1,212.0	692	1.75
Total	2,442.3	4,564	0.52

(*a*) See note, table 11.

TABLE 19
AVERAGE NUMBER OF MOW CULTIVATED PER PERSON AMONG DIFFERENT PEASANT CLASSES
(Ten Representative Villages in the District of Pan-yu, 1933)

Peasant Class	Mow Cultivated	Number of Persons	Average Mow Per Person
Poor	3,055.7	2,686	1.14

Peasant Class	Mow Cultivated	Number of Persons	Average Mow Per Person
Middle	2,267.3	944	2.40
Rich	2,733.0	692	3.95
Total	8,056.0	4,322	1.86

TABLE 20
VILLAGE FAMILIES CLASSIFIED
(Ten Representative Villages in the District of Pan-yu, 1933)

Class	Number of Families	Per Cent of Total
Landlords(a)	35	2.9
Rich Peasants	107	8.8
Middle Peasants	193	16.0
Poor Peasants	540	44.7
Agricultural Labourers	83	6.9
Others	251	20.7
Total	1,209	100.0

(a) Only the residential individual landlord families in the villages.

TABLE 21
LAND OWNED BY LANDLORDS AND PEASANTS
(Villages of Kang-sin and Kiu-tseng, 1933)

Class	Irrigated		Non-irrigated	
	Mow	Per Cent.	Mow	Per Cent.
Landlord	94.1(a)	61.3	59.5(a)	38.7
Rich Peasant	77.0	63.0	45.3	37.0
Middle Peasant	115.8	53.6	100.0	46.4

(a) Only those owned by individual and residential landlords.

Class	Irrigated		Non-irrigated	
	Mow	Mow	Per Cent.	Per Cent.
Poor Peasant	78.8	37.3	132.5	62.7
Total	365.7	52.0	337.3	48.0

TABLE 22

FORMS OF RENT PAYMENT IN RICE VILLAGES AND IN VILLAGES WITH
OTHER MAIN CROPS

(Eight Representative Villages in the District of Pan-yu, 1933)

Villages	Mow Under Tenancy	Rent in Rice		Rent in Money	
		Mow	Per Cent	Mow	Per Cent
Four Rice Villages(*a*)	3,459.1	1,802.2	52.1	1,656.9	47.9
Four Villages of Other Main Crops(*b*)	1,254.8	44.9	3.6	1,209.9	96.4
Total	4,713.9	1,847.1	39.2	2,866.8	60.8

(*a*) Nan-pu, Mei-tien, Ting-lung-fong, and Sha-dien-kong.
(*b*) Lung-tien, Pei-shan, Kong-sing, and Kwei-tien.

TABLE 23

FORMS OF RENT PAYMENT ACCORDING TO CLASS OF PEASANTS

(Ten Representative Villages of the District of Pan-yu, 1933)

Peasant Class	Mow under Tenancy	Rent in Rice		Rent in Money	
		Mow	Per Cent	Mow	Per Cent
Rich	1,617.5	273.0	16.9	1,344.5	83.1
Middle	1,594.3	732.2	45.9	862.1	54.1
Poor	2,530.7	1,281.9	50.7	1,248.8	49.3
Total	5,742.5	2,287.1	39.8	3,455.4	60.2

APPENDIX

TABLE 24
FALL IN PRICES OF FIVE AGRICULTURAL PRODUCTS
(Ten Representative Villages of the District of Pan-yu, 1928 and 1933)

Product	Price		Index for 1933 (1928=100)
	1928	1933	
Rice	7.00	4.50	64
Peanut	5.20	4.40	85
Potato	1.60	0.80	50
Taro	2.00	1.50	75
Turnip	1.00	0.50	50

TABLE 25A
NUMBER AND PROPORTION OF FAMILIES OF DIFFERENT CLASSES IN DEBT (a)
(Ten Representative Villages of the District of Pan-yu, 1933)

	Landlords (b)	Peasants			Agricultural Labourers	Total	Others	Grand Total
		Rich	Middle	Poor				
Total Number of Families	35	107	193	540	83	958	251	1,209
Number of Families in Debt	2	52	102	318	19	493	38	531
Per Cent of Families in Debt	5.7	48.6	52.8	58.9	22.9	51.4	15.1	43.9
Total Indebtedness (Yuan)	700	23,904	19,810	53,354	1,592	99,360	5,313	104,673
Average Indebtedness per Family (Yuan)	20.0	223.4	102.6	98.8	19.2	103.7	21.2	86.6

(a) Since almost none of the debts are incurred to capitalize the farming business with the exception of those of a few "rich" peasants, the term "in debt" may here be read as synonymous with "borrower."

(b) Not including corporate landlords.

APPENDIX

TABLE 25B

NUMBER AND PROPORTION OF PEASANT FAMILIES IN DEBT

(Fifteen Villages of Hwa-hsien, a District North of Pan-yu, 1934)

Village	Number of Families	Number of Families in Debt	Per Cent
S-sian	170	153	90
Shu-ling	300	200	66.6
Siao-pu-li	300	120	40
Ping-shan-liang	160	64	40
Li-pei	240	144	60
Yang-o-tseng	700	350	50
Ma-chi	450	360	80
Tien-mei	792	554	70
Wen-dan-kien	185	56	30
Ya-wu	405	284	70
Long-tu	540	432	80
Shi-ku	200	140	70
Sho-kiang-tang	427	299	70
Lian-tang	500	250	50
Sin-chuan	45	30	66.6
Total	5,414	3,436	63.4

TABLE 26
PROPORTION OF LAND MORTGAGED DURING FIVE YEARS, 1928-1933
(Ten Representative Villages of the District of Pan-yu)

Peasant Class	Mow owned in 1928	Mow mortgaged during 1928-1933	Per Cent of Area Mortgaged
Poor	521.8	28.1	5.4
Middle	765.3	27.4	3.6
Rich	1,289.2	62.0	4.8
Total	2,576.3	117.5	4.6

TABLE 27
COMPARISON OF NUMBER OF LABOURERS HIRED BY DIFFERENT PEASANT CLASSES
(Ten Representative Villages of Pan-yu, 1933)

Peasant Class	Per Cent of Families	Per Cent of Day-Labourers Hired	Per Cent of Yearly-Labourers Hired
Poor	64.3	15.2	—
Middle	23.0	16.5	—
Rich	12.7	68.3	100.0
Total	100.0	100.0	100.0

TABLE 28
COMPARISON OF HIRED LABOUR POWER USED BY DIFFERENT PEASANT CLASSES

Peasant Class	Number of Families	Mow Cultivated	Units of Day Labour per Day per Family	Units of Year Labour per Year per Family	Average Number of Units of Day Labour per Family	Average Number of Units of Day Labour per Mow Cultivated	Average Number of Units of Year Labour per Family
Poor	540	3,055.7	2,355	—	4.4	0.8	—
Middle	193	2,267.3	2,192	—	11.4	1.0	—
Rich	107	2,733.0	10,585	76	98.9	3.9	0.7
Total	840	8,056.0	15,132	76	16.1	1.9	0.1

APPENDIX

TABLE 29

COMPARISON OF HIRED LABOUR POWER USED IN RICE- AND FRUIT-GROWING REGIONS

(Five Villages of the District of Pan-yu, 1933)

Peasant Class	Average Number of Units of Day Labour per Family		Average Number of Units of Day Labour per Mow Cultivated		Average Number of Units of Year Labour per Family	
	Rice(a)	Fruit(b)	Rice	Fruit	Rice	Fruit
Rich	68.8	151.0	2.49	5.41	0.17	1.61
Middle	17.0	19.4	1.24	2.86	—	—
Poor	6.9	2.2	1.06	0.77	—	—
Total	16.1	44.2	1.55	4.36	0.02	0.42

(a) Three rice-growing villages: Mei-tien, Nan-pu, and Sha-dien-kong.
(b) Two fruit-growing villages: Pei-shan and Lung-tien.

TABLE 30

COMPARISON OF WAGES EARNED BY MALE AND FEMALE AGRICULTURAL LABOURERS

(Ten Representative Villages of Pan-yu, 1933)

Agricultural Labourers			Wages		
			Minimum	Maximum	Average
Year Labourers, rate (Yuan, per annum)			60.0	160.0	100.0
Day Labourers (Yuan, per day)	in busy seasons	Male	0.5	1.8	1.0
		Female	0.3	0.8	0.6
	at ordinary times	Male	0.3	0.8	0.5
		Female	0.2	0.4	0.3

APPENDIX

TABLE 31
LANDLORD AND PEASANT FAMILIES WHOSE MEMBERS HAVE VOCATIONS OTHER THAN IN AGRICULTURE
(Ten Representative Villages of Pan-yu, 1933)

Class	No. of Families with Members Whose Vocation is Outside Agriculture	Such Members Engaged					
		as Coolies, Soldiers, Peddlers, or Shopkeepers		in a Profession (b)		in Industry, Trade, Civil or Military Official Positions	
		Number	Per Cent	Number	Per Cent	Number	Per Cent
Landlords(a)	15	7	46.7	6	40.0	2	13.3
Rich	62	50	80.7	11	17.7	1	1.6
Middle	107	103	96.3	4	3.7	—	—
Poor	350	344	98.3	6	1.7	—	—
Agricultural Labourers	54	54	100.0	—	—	—	—
Total	588	558	94.9	27	4.6	3	0.5

(a) Only individual residential landlords.

(b) Including not only occupations recognized as professional in Western lands but also letter-writing, fortune-telling, ceremonial occupations, the lesser forms of teaching, etc.

APPENDIX

TABLE 32

THE CHANGE IN ECONOMIC STATUS FOR THE FAMILIES OF ALL CLASSES(a)

(Ten Representative Villages of the District of Pan-yu, 1928 to 1933)

Class	No. of Families in 1928	Number of Families in 1933 — Landlords(b)	Rich Peasants	Middle Peasants	Poor Peasants	Agricultural Labourers	Others	Emigrants	Total	No. of Families Increased Through Property Division
		35	107	193	540	83	251			
Immigrant							1		1	
Others	252	3	2	4	23	2	223		257	5
Agricultural Labourers	82				4	73	3	2	82	
Poor Peasants	493		1	2	480	6	13	1	503	10
Middle Peasants	202		8	170	29	2			218	16
Rich Peasants	109	4	95	16	4		2		121	12
Landlords(b)	30	28	1	1					30	

(a) In this table the figures on the dotted line represent the families whose economic position has not much changed during the five years under review. Except those under the item "others," the figures above this dotted line represent the families whose economic position has risen, and the figures below it indicate the families whose economic position has worsened during the same period.

(b) Only individual residential landlords.

138

APPENDIX

TABLE 33

CHANGE IN THE PROPORTION OF FAMILIES OF THE DIFFERENT ECONOMIC CLASSES
(Ten Representative Villages in the District of Pan-yu, 1928 and 1933)

Class	Per Cent in Total Number of Families		Index for 1933 (1928 = 100)
	1928	1933	
Landlords(a)	2.6	2.9	111.5
Rich Peasants	9.3	8.8	94.6
Middle Peasants	17.3	16.0	92.5
Poor Peasants	42.2	44.7	105.9
Agricultural Labourers	7.0	6.9	98.6
Others	21.6	20.7	95.8
Total	100.0	100.0	—

(a) Only individual and residential landlords.

TABLE 34

VOCATIONS OF HEADS OF FAMILIES NOT MAINLY SUPPORTED BY AGRICULTURE
(LANDLORDS AND PEASANTS)
(Ten Representative Villages in the District of Pan-yu, 1933)

Vocations	Number of Families	Percentage of Total Number of Non-Agricultural Families
Coolies, soldiers, peddlers, shop-keepers	177	72.2
In a profession(a)	45	18.4
In Industry, trade, civil or military official positions	23	9.4
Total	245(b)	100.0

(a) See note to Table 31.
(b) Six families have been excluded because their vocations are not exactly known.

APPENDIX

TABLE 35
PRESENT VOCATIONS OF PEASANT FAMILIES EMIGRATED DURING THE LAST TWENTY YEARS
(Ten Representative Villages in the District of Pan-yu, 1933)

Vocations	Number of Families	Percentage of Total Number of Non-Agricultural Families
In industry, trade, civil or military official positions, and professions	—	—
In agriculture	25	30.5
Coolies, soldiers, peddlers, shopkeepers	57	69.5
Total	82	100.0

INDEX

A

Production, agricultural, decline of, 2, 3, 97, 98.
Products, chief, Area devoted to, 129, 130.
Purchase, length of periods for, 62.

R

Remittances, from overseas, 67, 71, 84, 85, 91.
Rents, collection of, 44, 61, 63.
  „ payment of, in Rice Villages, 132.
  „ payment of, according to class of peasants, 132.
  „ , High, 66.
  „ , in cash, 48, 49, 54, 55, 56, 63, 66.
  „ , income from, 24, 25, 36.
  „ , increase or reduction of, 67, 68.
  „ , in grain, 48, 54, 55, 56, 59, 60, 61, 62.
  „ , payable in advance, 44, 48.
  „ , Share, 57, 58, 59.
  „ , selling of children to pay, 60, 61, 62, 95.
Requisitions, by military, 79.
Responsibility, family, 31.
Rice Cultivation, 6, 14, 15, 16, 103.
Rice, and Fruit growing, hired labour used by, 136.
  „ and Fruit, income from, 48.
  „ production, cost, 12, 14, 15, 16.
  „ „ , Japan and China, comparison, 14.
Rights, Shore, disputes over, 64.
Road-Building, assessment for, 76, 77, 78, 79.

S

Self-government, rural, 40, 41.
Sha-kuo-chuan, 63, 64, 75.
Sha-tien, 22, 29, 30, 75, 81.

Siao-wu, 57, 58.
Silk, and cocoons, price of, 66.
Social Organizations, land of, 25, 26.
Sources of Income, Auxiliary, 108, 109.
Speculation, commercial, 55.
Status, economic, change in, 138.
  „ „ change in proportion, 139.

T

Taxes, collection of, 40, 74, 75.
  „ , Land and Dyke, 59, 81, 82, 83.
  „ , Various, 73, 74, 79, 80.
Tenancy, hereditary, 51, 52, 53, 57, 58.
  „ , system of, 42, 43, 46.
Tenants, proportion of, 3, 4.
Transfers, of lease, 51, 52.
Tsan-kao, 29.
Tso-ke, system of, 59, 60.

U

Usury, 92, 93, 94, 95.

V

Village, families classified, 131.
Villages, statistics of cultivation, 12.
  „ , Survey of, 2.
Villages, Rice, rent payment by, 132.
Vocations, of Peasant families emigrated, 140.

W

Wages, 47, 48, 98, 99, 100, 101, 102, 103, 104, 105.
Wealth, concentration of, 18, 20.